From th

Welcome to our extra-special new astrological forecast which takes you up to the end of the century on Dec our year-ahead guides all the astrolo; tables and a calculator. Today, by the miracle of computers, we have to build our knowledge and hard work into a program which calculates the precise astrological aspect for every day in a flash.

When Shakespeare wrote 'The fault, dear Brutus, is not in our stars, but in ourselves', he spoke for every astrologer. In our day-to-day forecasts we cannot hope to be 100% accurate every time, because this would remove the most important influence in your life, which is you! What we can hope to do is to give you a sense of the astrological backdrop to the day, week or month in question, and so prompt you to think a little harder about what is going in your own life, and thus help improve your chances of acting effectively to deal with events and situations.

During the course of a year, there may be one or two readings that are similar in nature. This is not an error, it is simply that the Moon or a planet has repeated a particular pattern. In addition, a planetary pattern that applies to your sign may apply to someone else's sign at some other point during the year. One planetary 'return' that you already know well is the Solar return that occurs every year on your birthday.

If you've read our guides before, you'll know that we're never less than positive and that our advice is unpretentious, down to earth, and rooted in daily experience. If this is the first time you've met us, please regard us not as in any way astrological gurus, but as good friends who wish you nothing but health, prosperity and contentment. Happy 1998-9!

Sasha Fenton is a world-renowned astrologer, palmist and Tarot card reader, with over 80 books published on Astrology, Palmistry, Tarot and other forms of divination. Now living in London, Sasha is a regular broadcaster on radio and television, as well as making frequent contributions to newspapers and magazines around the world, including South Africa and Australia. She is a former President and Secretary of the British Astrological and Psychic Society (BAPS) and Secretary of the Advisory Panel on Astrological Education.

Jonathan Dee is an astrologer, artist and historian based in Wales, and a direct descendant of the great Elizabethan alchemist and wizard Dr John Dee, court astrologer to Queen Elizabeth I. He has written a number of books, including the recently completed *The Chronicles of Ancient Egypt,* and for the last five years has co-written an annual astrological forecast series with Sasha Fenton. A regular broadcaster on television and radio, he has also hosted the Starline show for KQED Talk Radio, New Mexico.

YOUR DAY-BY-DAY FORECAST
SEPTEMBER 1998 – DECEMBER 1999

SASHA FENTON • JONATHAN DEE

HALDANE • MASON

Zambezi

DEDICATION

For the memory of Gary Bailey, a new star in heaven.

ACKNOWLEDGEMENTS

With many thanks to our computer wizard, Sean Lovatt.

———————————————————

This edition published 1998
by Haldane Mason Ltd
59 Chepstow Road
London W2 5BP

ISBN 1-902463-07-2

Designed and produced by Haldane Mason Ltd
Cover illustration by Lo Cole
Edited by Jan Budkowski

Printed in Singapore by Craft Print Pte Ltd

CONTENTS

An Astrological Overview of the 20th Century

Next year the shops will be full of astrology books for the new century and also for the new millennium. In this book, the last of the old century, we take a brief look back to see where the slow-moving outer planets were in each decade and what it meant. Obviously this will be no more than a very brief glance backwards but next year you will be able to see the picture in much more depth when we bring out our own book for the new millennium.

1900 – 1909

The century began with Pluto in Gemini and it was still in Gemini by the end of the decade. Neptune started out in Gemini but moved into cancer in 1901 and ended the decade still in Cancer. Uranus started the century in Sagittarius, moving to Capricorn in 1904 and ending the decade still in Capricorn. Saturn began the century in Sagittarius, moving to Capricorn in January 1900 and then through Aquarius, Pisces and Aries, ending the decade in Aries.

The stars and the decade

In general terms, the planet of upheaval in the dynastic sign of Sagittarius with Saturn also in that sign and Pluto opposing it, all at the very start of the century put the spotlight on dynasties, royalty and empires. As Saturn left for the 'establishment' sign of Capricorn these just about held together but as the decade ended, the power and control that these ancient dynasties had were loosening their grip on the developed world of the time. Queen Victoria died in 1901 and her son, Edward VII was dying by the end of the decade, so in Britain, the Victorian age of certainty was already coming to an end. The Boer War was only just won by Britain in 1902 which brought a shock to this successful colonial country.

Pluto in Gemini brought a transformation in methods of communications. It was as Saturn entered the innovative sign of Aquarius that these took concrete and useful form. Thus it was during this decade that the motor car, telephone, typewriter, gramophone and colour photography came into existence. Air travel began in 1900 with the first Zeppelin airship flight, the first powered aeroplane flight by the Wright brothers in 1904 and Louis Blériot's flight across the English Channel in 1909. Edison demonstrated the Kinetophone, the first machine capable of showing talking moving pictures in

1910. Even the nature of war changed as technologically modern Japan managed to fight off the might of the Russian empire in the war of 1904 - 1905.

The Treaty of Versailles, followed by further treaties of Aix and Trianon served to crush the German nation and therefore sow the seeds of the next war.

1910 - 1919

Pluto opened the decade in Gemini, moving to Cancer in 1913. Neptune travelled from Cancer to Leo in September 1914 while Uranus moved out of Capricorn, through Aquarius to end the decade in Pisces. Saturn moved from Aries to Taurus, then to Gemini, back into Taurus, then into Gemini again entering Cancer in 1914, then on through Leo and ending the decade in Virgo.

The stars and the decade

Now we see the start of a pattern. Sagittarius may be associated with dynasties but it is the home-loving and patriotic signs of Cancer and Leo that actually seem to be associated with major wars. The desire either to expand a country's domestic horizons or to protect them from the expansion of others is ruled by the maternal sign of Cancer, followed by the paternal one of Leo. Home, family, tradition, safety all seem to be fought over when major planets move through these signs. When future generations learn about the major wars of the 20th century they will probably be lumped together in their minds - despite the 20-year gap between them - just as we lump the Napoleonic wars together, forgetting that there was a nine-year gap between them, and of course, this long stay of Pluto in Cancer covered the whole of this period.

It is interesting to note that Pluto moved into Cancer in July 1913 and Neptune entered Leo on the 23rd of September 1914, just three of weeks after the outbreak of the First World War. Saturn moved into Cancer in April 1914. Pluto is associated with transformation, Neptune with dissolution and Saturn with loss, sadness and sickness. Many people suffered and so many families and dynasties were unexpectedly dissolved at that time, among these, the Romanov Czar and his family and the kings of Portugal, Hungary, Italy and Germany and the Manchu dynasty of China. America (born on the 4th of July, 1776 and therefore a Cancerian country) was thrust into prominence as a major economic and social power after this war. Russia experienced the Bolshevik revolution during it. As Saturn moved into Virgo (the sign that is associated with health) at the end of this decade, a world-wide plague of influenza killed 20 million people, far more than had died during the course of the war itself.

CANCER

1920 – 1929

The roaring 20s began and ended with Pluto in Cancer. Neptune moved from Leo to Virgo at the end of this decade and Uranus moved from Pisces to Aries in 1927. Saturn travelled from Virgo, through Libra, Scorpio, Sagittarius and then backwards and forwards between Sagittarius and Capricorn, ending up in Capricorn at the end of 1929.

The stars and the decade

Pluto's long transformative reign in Cancer made life hard for men during this time. Cancer is the most female of all the signs, being associated with nurturing and motherhood. Many men were sick in mind and body as a result of the war and women began to take proper jobs for the first time. Family planning and better living conditions brought improvements in life for ordinary people and in the developed world there was a major boom in house building as well as in improved road and rail commuter systems. The time of lords and ladies was passing and ordinary people were demanding better conditions. Strikes and unrest were common, especially in Germany. As the decade ended, the situation both domestically and in the foreign policies of the developed countries began to look up. Even the underdeveloped countries began to modernize a little. Shortly before the middle of this decade, all the politicians who might have prevented the rise of Hitler and the Nazi party died and then came the stock market crash of 1929. The probable astrological sequence that set this train of circumstances off was the run up to the opposition of Saturn in Capricorn to Pluto in Cancer which took place in 1931. The effects of such major planetary events are often felt while the planets are closing into a conjunction or opposition etc., rather than just at the time of their exactitude.

On a brighter note great strides were made in the worlds of art, music and film and ordinary people could enjoy more entertainment than ever before, in 1929 the first colour television was demonstrated and in 1928 Alexander Fleming announced his discovery of penicillin. At the very start of the decade prohibition passed into US Federal law, ushering in the age of organized crime and as a spin-off a great increase in drinking in that country and later on, all those wonderful gangster films. The same year, the partition of Ireland took place bringing more conflict and this time on a very long-term basis.

1930 – 1939

The 1930s should have been better than the 1920s but they were not. Pluto remained in Cancer until 1937, Neptune remained in Virgo throughout the decade, Uranus entered Taurus in 1934 and Saturn moved from Capricorn through Aquarius, Pisces then back and forth between Aries and Pisces, ending the decade in Taurus.

The stars and the decade

Neptune's voyage through Virgo did help in the field of advances in medicine and in public health. Pluto continued to make life hard for men and then by extension for families, while in the 'motherhood' sign of Cancer. While Saturn was in the governmental signs of Capricorn and Aquarius, democracy ceased to exist anywhere in the world. In the UK a coalition government was in power for most of the decade while in the USA, Franklin Delano Roosevelt ruled as a kind of benign emperor for almost three terms of office, temporarily dismantling much of that country's democratic machinery while he did so. Governments in Russia, Germany, Italy, Spain and Japan moved to dictatorships or dictatorial types of government with all the resultant tyranny, while France, Britain and even the USA floundered for much of the time. China was ruled by warring factions. However, there was an upsurge of popular entertainment at this time, especially through the mediums of film, music and radio probably due to the advent of adventurous, inventive Uranus into the music and entertainment sign of Taurus in 1934.

1940 – 1949

War years once again. Pluto remained in the 'paternal' sign of Leo throughout this decade, bringing tyranny and control of the masses in all the developed countries and also much of the Third World. Neptune entered Libra in 1942, Uranus moved from Taurus to Gemini in 1941, then to Cancer in 1948. Saturn began the decade in Taurus, moved to Gemini, Cancer, Leo and finally Virgo during this decade. The 'home and country' signs of Cancer and Leo were once more thrust into the limelight in a war context. Neptune is not a particularly warlike planet and Libra is normally a peaceable sign but Libra does rule open enemies as well as peace and harmony.

The stars and the decade

To continue looking for the moment at the planet Neptune, astrologers don't take its dangerous side seriously enough. Neptune can use the sea in a particularly destructive manner when it wants to with tidal waves, disasters at sea and so on, so it is interesting to note that the war in the West was almost lost for the allies at sea due to the success of the German U-boats. Hitler gambled on a quick end to the war in the east and shut his mind to Napoleon's experience of the Russian winter. Saturn through Cancer and Leo, followed by the inventive sign of Uranus entering Cancer at the end of the decade almost brought home, family, tradition and the world itself to an end with the explosions of the first atomic bombs.

However, towards the end of this decade, it became clear that democracy, the rights of ordinary people and a better lifestyle for everybody were a better answer than trying to find 'lebensraum' by pinching one's neighbour's land and enslaving its population. Saturn's entry into Virgo brought great advances in medicine and the plagues and diseases of the past began to diminish throughout the world. Pluto in Leo transformed the power structures of every country and brought such ideas as universal education, better housing and social security systems - at least in the developed world.

1950 - 1959

Pluto still dipped in and out of Leo until it finally left for Virgo in 1957. Neptune finally left Libra for Scorpio in 1955, Uranus sat on that dangerous and warlike cusp of Cancer and Leo, while Saturn moved swiftly through Virgo, Libra, Scorpio, Sagittarius and then into Capricorn.

The stars and the decade

The confrontations between dictators and between dictatorships and democracy continued during this time with the emphasis shifting to the conflict between communism and capitalism. The Korean war started the decade and the communist take-over in China ended it. Military alertness was reflected in the UK by the two years of national service that young men were obliged to perform throughout the decade. Rationing, shortages of food, fuel and consumer goods remained in place for half the decade, but by the end of it, the world was becoming a very different place. With American money, Germany and Japan were slowly rebuilt, communism did at least bring a measure of stability in China and the Soviet Union, although its pervasive power brought fear and peculiar witch hunts in the United States. In Europe and the USA the lives of ordinary people improved beyond belief.

Pluto in Virgo brought plenty of work for the masses and for ordinary people, poverty began to recede for the first time in history. Better homes, labour-saving devices and the vast amount of popular entertainment in the cinema, the arts, popular music and television at long last brought fun into the lives of most ordinary folk. In Britain and the Commonwealth, in June 1953, the coronation of the new Queen ushered in a far more optimistic age while her Empire dissolved around her.

C A N C E R

1960 – 1969

This is the decade that today's middle-aged folk look back on with fond memories, yet it was not always as safe as we like to think. Pluto remained in Virgo throughout the decade bringing work and better health to many people. Neptune remained in Scorpio throughout this time, while Uranus traversed back and forth between Leo and Virgo, then from Virgo to Libra, ending the decade in Libra. Saturn hovered around the cusp of Taurus and Gemini until the middle of the decade and then on through Gemini and Cancer, spending time around the Cancer/Leo cusp and then on through Leo to rest once again on the Leo/Virgo cusp.

The stars and the decade

The Cancer/Leo threats of atomic war were very real in the early 1960s, with the Cuban missile crisis bringing America and the Soviet Union to the point of war. The Berlin wall went up. President Kennedy's assassination in November 1963 shocked the world and the atmosphere of secrets, spies and mistrust abounded in Europe, the USA and in the Soviet Union. One of the better manifestations of this time of cold war, CIA dirty tricks and spies was the plethora of wonderful spy films and television programmes of the early 60s. Another was the sheer fun of the Profumo affair!

The late 1960s brought the start of a very different atmosphere. The Vietnam War began to be challenged by the teenagers whose job it was to die in it and the might of America was severely challenged by these tiny Vietcong soldiers in black pyjamas and sandals. The wave of materialism of the 1950s was less attractive to the flower-power generation of the late 60s. The revolutionary planet Uranus in balanced Libra brought the protest movement into being and an eventual end to racial segregation in the USA. Equality between the sexes was beginning to be considered. The troubles of Northern Ireland began at the end of this decade.

In 1969, Neil Armstrong stepped out onto the surface of the Moon, thereby marking the start of a very different age, the New Age, the Age of Aquarius.

1970 – 1979

Pluto began the decade around the Virgo/Libra cusp, settling in Libra in 1972 and remaining there for the rest of the decade. Neptune started the decade by moving back and forth between Scorpio and Sagittarius and residing in Sagittarius for the rest of the decade. Uranus hovered between Libra and Scorpio until 1975 and then travelled through Scorpio until the end of the decade while Saturn moved from Taurus to Gemini, then hung around the Cancer/Leo cusp and finally moved into Virgo.

The stars and the decade

The planets in or around that dangerous Cancer/Leo cusp and the continuing Libran emphasis brought more danger from total war as America struggled with Vietnam and the cold war. However, the influence of Virgo brought work, an easier life and more hope than ever to ordinary people in the First World. Uranus in Libra brought different kinds of love partnerships into public eye as fewer people bothered to marry. Divorce became easier and homosexuality became legal. With Uranus opening the doors to secretive Scorpio, spies such as Burgess, Maclean, Philby, Lonsdale and Penkowski began to come in from the cold. President Nixon was nicely caught out at Watergate, ushering in a time of more openness in governments everywhere.

If you are reading this book, you may be doing so because you are keen to know about yourself and your sign, but you are likely to be quite interested in astrology and perhaps in other esoteric techniques. You can thank the atmosphere of the 1970s for the openness and the lack of fear and superstition which these subjects now enjoy. The first festival of Mind, Body and Spirit took place in 1976 and the British Astrological and Psychic Society was launched in the same year, both of these events being part of the increasing interest in personal awareness and alternative lifestyles.

Neptune in Scorpio brought fuel crises and Saturn through Cancer and Leo brought much of the repression of women to an end, with some emancipation from tax and social anomalies. Tea bags and instant coffee allowed men for the first time to cope with the terrible hardship of making a cuppa!

1980 - 1989

Late in 1983, Pluto popped into the sign of Scorpio, popped out again and re-entered it in 1984. Astrologers of the 60s and 70s feared this planetary situation in case it brought the ultimate Plutonic destruction with it. Instead of this, the Soviet Union and South Africa freed themselves from tyranny and the Berlin Wall came down. The main legacy of Pluto in Scorpio is the Scorpionic association of danger through sex, hence the rise of AIDS. Neptune began the decade in Sagittarius then it travelled back and forth over the Sagittarius/Capricorn cusp, ending the decade in Capricorn. Uranus moved from Scorpio, back and forth over the Scorpio/Sagittarius cusp, then through Sagittarius, ending the decade in Capricorn. Saturn began the decade in Virgo, then hovered around the Virgo/Libra cusp, through Libra, Scorpio and Sagittarius, resting along the Sagittarius/Capricorn cusp, ending the decade in Capricorn.

The stars and the decade
The movement of planets through the dynastic sign of Sagittarius brought doubt and uncertainty to Britain's royal family, while the planets in authoritative Capricorn brought strong government to the UK in the form of Margaret Thatcher. Ordinary people began to seriously question the *status quo* and to attempt to change it. Even in the hidden empire of China, modernization and change began to creep in. Britain went to war again by sending the gunboats to the Falkland Islands to fight off a truly old-fashioned takeover bid by the daft Argentinean dictator, General Galtieri.

Saturn is an earth planet, Neptune rules the sea, while Uranus is associated with the air. None of these planets was in their own element and this may have had something to do with the increasing number of natural and man-made disasters that disrupted the surface of the earth during this decade. The first space shuttle flight took place in 1981 and the remainder of the decade reflected many people's interest in extra-terrestrial life in the form of films and television programmes. ET went home. Black rap music and the casual use of drugs became a normal part of the youth scene. Maybe the movement of escapist Neptune through the 'outer space' sign of Sagittarius had something to do with this.

1990 - 1999
Pluto began the decade in Scorpio, moving in and out of Sagittarius until 1995 remaining there for the rest of the decade. Neptune began the decade in Capricorn, travelling back and forth over the cusp of Aquarius, ending the decade in Aquarius, Uranus moved in and out of Aquarius, remaining there from 1996 onwards. Saturn travelled from Capricorn, through Aquarius, Pisces (and back again), then on through Pisces, Aries, in and out of Taurus, finally ending the decade in Taurus.

The stars and the decade
The Aquarian emphasis has brought advances in science and technology and a time when computers are common even in the depths of darkest Africa. The logic and fairness of Aquarius does seem to have affected many of the peoples of the earth. Pluto in the open sign of Sagittarius brought much governmental secrecy to an end, it will also transform the traditional dynasties of many countries before it leaves them for good. The aftermath of the dreadful and tragic death of Princess Diana in 1997 put a rocket under the creaking 19th-century habits of British royalty.

The final decade began with yet another war – this time the Gulf War – which sent a serious signal to all those who fancy trying their hand at international bullying or the 19th-century tactics of pinching your neighbour's land and resources. Uranus's last fling in Capricorn tore up the earth with volcanoes and earthquakes, and its stay in Aquarius seems to be keeping this pattern going. Saturn in Pisces, opposite the 'health' sign of Virgo is happily bringing new killer viruses into being and encouraging old ones to build up resistance to antibiotics. The bubonic plague is alive and well in tropical countries along with plenty of other plagues that either are, or are becoming resistant to modern medicines. Oddly enough the planetary line-up in 1997 was similar to that of the time of the great plague of London in 1665!

Films, the arts, architecture all showed signs of beginning an exciting period of revolution in 1998. Life became more electronic and computer-based for the younger generation while in the old world, the vast army of the elderly began to struggle with a far less certain world of old-age poverty and strange and frightening innovations. Keeping up to date and learning to adapt is the only way to survive now, even for the old folks.

It is interesting to note that the first event of importance to shock Europe in this century was the morganatic marriage of Franz Ferdinand, the heir to the massively powerful Austro-Hungarian throne. This took place in the summer of 1900. The unpopularity of this controlling and repressive empire fell on its head in Sarajevo on the 28th of July 1914. This mighty empire is now almost forgotten, but its death throes are still being played out in and around Sarajevo today - which only goes to show how long it can take for anything to be settled.

Technically the twentieth century only ends at the beginning of the year 2001 but most of us will be celebrating the end of the century and the end of the millennium and the end of the last day of 1999 - that is if we are all here of course! A famous prediction of global disaster comes from the writings of the French writer, doctor and astrologer Nostradamus (1503–66):

- The year 1999, seventh month,
- From the sky will come a great King of Terror:
- To bring back to life the great King of the Mongols,
- Before and after Mars reigns.
  (Quatrain X:72 from the *Centuries*)

Jonathan has worked out that with the adjustments of the calendar from the time of Nostradamus, the date of the predicted disaster will be the 11th of August 1999. As it happens there will be a total eclipse of the Sun at ten past eleven on that day at 18 degrees of Leo. We have already seen how the signs of Cancer, Leo and Libra seem to be the ones that are most clearly associated with war and this reference to 'Mars reigning' is the fact that Mars is the god of war. Therefore, the prediction suggests that an Oriental king will wage a war from the sky that brings terror to the world. Some people have suggested that this event would bring about the end of the world but that is not what the prediction actually says. A look back over the 1900s has proved this whole century to be one of terror from the skies but it would be awful to think that there would be yet another war, this time emanating from Mongolia. Terrible but not altogether impossible to imagine I guess. Well, let us hope that we are all here for us to write and for you to enjoy the next set of zodiac books for the turn of the millennium and beyond.

2000 onwards: a very brief look forward

The scientific exploration and eventual colonization of space is on the way now. Scorpio rules fossil fuels and there will be no major planets passing through this sign for quite a while so alternative fuel sources will have to be sought. Maybe it will be the entry of Uranus into the pioneering sign of Aries in January 2012 that will make a start on this. The unusual line up of the 'ancient seven' planets of Sun, Moon, Mercury, Venus, Mars and Saturn in Taurus on the 5th of May 2000 will be interesting. Taurus represents such matters as land, farming, building, cooking, flowers, the sensual beauty of music, dancing and the arts. Jonathan and Sasha will work out the astrological possibilities for the future in depth and put out ideas together for you in a future book.

The Essential Cancer

YOUR RULING PLANET Your ruling body is the Moon. The Moon represents the feminine principle, associated with travel, the sea and the goddess Persephone, sometimes known as Selene. The Moon is also associated with Diana, the virgin huntress, twin sister of Apollo.

YOUR SYMBOL The crab is the symbol for your sign. The crab has a hard shell and a soft and tasty interior, just like you. It also goes about things in a sideways direction, which you also do on occasion. Legend has it that the crab was thrown into the sky for pinching Hercules on the toe while he was carrying out one of his testing labours.

PARTS OF THE BODY The lungs, breast and rib cage, also the stomach and digestive organs.

YOUR GOOD BITS You are a good listener and a kind-hearted and sympathetic friend. Your family relies upon you.

YOUR BAD BITS You can be moody and bad-tempered without being able to explain why. You can cling to your family.

YOUR WEAKNESSES You worry about everything, especially money.

YOUR BEST DAY Monday. This is the Moon's day.

YOUR WORST DAY Wednesday.

YOUR COLOURS White, silver and all pearly or oyster colours.

CITIES Amsterdam, Manchester, Venice, New York, Christchurch.

COUNTRIES Scotland, Holland, Mauritius, New Zealand. Although some astrologers suggest Gemini or even Sagittarius for the USA, we believe that it's actually Cancer because the country was 'born' on the fourth of July!

HOLIDAYS Anywhere by or on water, especially the sea.

YOUR FAVOURITE CAR This would probably be an estate car that is large enough to hold the entire family, the dogs and all the shopping. If this isn't roomy enough, how about one of those twelve-seater buses?

YOUR FAVOURITE MEAL OUT You are an excellent cook and therefore a discriminating diner. You probably enjoy French food, created with the freshest ingredients and cooked to perfection. You wouldn't hesitate to ask for the recipe.

YOUR FAVOURITE DRINK Anything in a glass, preferably paid for by someone else!

YOUR HERBS Rosemary, comfrey.

YOUR TREES Traditionally willow, but also the mangrove because this also grows near or in water. In Australia, Sasha suggests the paperbark tree for much the same reason.

YOUR FLOWERS Acanthus, lotus (water lily) and wild flowers. As Cancerians have good memories, therefore rosemary for remembrance.

YOUR ANIMALS Crab, lobster, tortoise, owl, otter, cuckoo, frog.

YOUR METAL Silver.

YOUR GEMS The pearl, also mother-of-pearl.

MODE OF DRESS You favour rather formal clothes in attractive colours such as lavender or pale greens and blues.

YOUR CAREERS Small shopkeeper, antique dealer, teacher, nurse, carer, chef, hotelier, management.

YOUR FRIENDS Fairly gentle, home-loving types and also business people. Those who respect privacy.

YOUR ENEMIES Rude, brash, noisy and unhelpful people.

YOUR FAVOURITE GIFT Cancerians are supposed to be home-loving, and so you are – but you do love to get away on trips and holidays.

Tickets to an outing or any kind of event suits you nicely. You also love music, so tickets to a show or a pop concert would be good. Gadgets for the kitchen and nice tableware are also appreciated. You also love albums, silver ornaments, jewellery, antiques, coins, and other collectibles.

YOUR IDEAL HOME You like living in a happy family atmosphere. Otherwise, you enjoy living close to your family or near another family that you can become attached to. You prefer older buildings and when you find the right place, you tend to stay there for years. You may even add an extension for visiting friends and relatives.

YOUR FAVOURITE BOOKS Love stories, and those that are set in exotic locations.

YOUR FAVOURITE MUSIC Nostalgic music that brings back pleasant memories. Soft pop.

YOUR GAMES AND SPORTS Football, walking and exploring. You have an excellent memory, so games of strategy and card games such as poker appeal.

YOUR PAST AND FUTURE LIVES There are many theories about past lives and even some about future ones, but we suggest that your immediate past life was ruled by the sign previous to Cancer and that your future life will be governed by the sign that follows Cancer. Therefore you were Gemini in your previous life and will be Leo in the next. If you want to know all about either of these signs, zip straight out to the shops and buy our books on them!

YOUR LUCKY NUMBER Your lucky number is 4. To find your lucky number on a raffle ticket or something similar, first add the number s together. For example, if one of your lottery numbers is 28, add 2 + 8 to make 10; then add 1 + 0, to give the root number of 1. The number 316 on a raffle ticket works in the same way. Add 3 + 1 + 6 to make 10: then add 1 + 0, making 1. As your lucky numbers should add up to 4, numbers 4, 31, 211 or similar would work. A selection of lottery numbers should include some of the following: 4, 13, 22, 31, 40 and 49.

CANCER

Your Sun Sign

*Your Sun Sign is determined by your date of birth.
Thus anyone born between 21st March and 20th April is Aries and so
on through the calendar. Your Rising Sign (see page 36)
is determined by the day and time of your birth.*

CANCER

RULED BY THE MOON
22nd June to 23rd July

Cancer is a feminine, water sign whose symbol is the crab. This means you are sensitive, caring towards others and a bit moody and difficult at times. You have a kindly and sympathetic nature, take an interest in people and make a good listener. You enjoy chatting for hours and usually manage to find out lots about everyone around you, so you could make an excellent counsellor.

You may look soft on the outside but you have a strong, stubborn streak which comes to the fore if anyone tries to attack you or one of your family. Many of you are shrewd and clever business people, especially if there is any selling to be done, but you can be conned out of money, especially by those you love. Yours is a very domestic sign and you may be a very keen cook. You certainly like eating and drinking, but this is for the sheer pleasure of having something good, rather than from gluttony or the desire to get drunk.

Your faults are clannishness and a suspicion of outsiders. You may be selfish or penny-pinching in small ways and generous in big ones. However, if one of your children needs anything, you will pull out all the stops to make sure that they have it. Some of you are great animal lovers, while others enjoy watching wildlife documentaries without wanting to keep pets themselves. Your relatives can count on your support and your partner can lean on you when the going gets rough.

You may look backwards rather than forwards, enjoying looking over family albums and talking about the old days. History fascinates you and you may collect objects which have a historical significance. You hate to throw anything away and you could have cupboards stuffed with any amount of old junk. ('You never know, dear, it might come in useful one day!')

You could be clingy with those you love, especially your children, and you may not want to travel too far away from them. If you can keep contact with children and in time, grandchildren, this makes you happy. Some of you try to live through a child in some way, encouraging him or her or do the things that you would have liked to do. There are some Cancerians who will do this with a partner, supporting their endeavours so that they can get close to the edge of excitement, glamour and achievement without having to do any of it themselves. You may be a pessimist or a worrier and you find it hard to bounce back from financial losses or hard times. It is always difficult for you to shake off the past, especially if any part of it is worrying or frightening, and you may be guilty of harping on at your partner about sins – in your eyes – committed many years ago. You may also fear change, and become attached to familiar surroundings. You need to have your personal belongings around you.

Despite being very fond of your home and your family, you love to travel. You see your home as a base but this doesn't mean that you don't enjoy leaving it behind from time to time. You love novelty and change of all kinds, especially a change of scene. A meal out with friends and a stimulating trip away is always well received.

All the Other Sun Signs

ARIES
21st March to 20th April

Ariens can get anything they want off the ground, but they may land back down again with a bump. Quick to think and to act, Ariens are often intelligent and have little patience with fools. This includes anyone who is slower than themselves.

They are not the tidiest of people and they are impatient with details, except when engaged upon their special subject; then Ariens can fiddle around for hours. They are willing to make huge financial sacrifices for their families and they can put up with relatives living with them as long as this leaves them free to do their own thing. Aries women are decisive and competitive at work but many are disinterested in homemaking. They might consider giving up a relationship if it interfered with their ambitions. Highly sexed and experimental, they are faithful while in love but, if love begins to fade, they start to look around. Ariens may tell themselves that they are only looking for amusement, but they may end up in a fulfilling relationship with someone else's partner. This kind of situation offers the continuity and emotional support which they need with no danger of boredom or entrapment.

Their faults are those of impatience and impetuosity, coupled with a hot temper. They can pick a furious row with a supposed adversary, tear him or her to pieces then walk away from the situation five minutes later, forgetting all about it. Unfortunately, the poor victim can't always shake off the effects of the row in quite the same way. However, Arien cheerfulness, spontaneous generosity and kindness make them the greatest friends to have.

TAURUS
21st April to 21st May

These people are practical and persevering. Taureans are solid and reliable, regular in habits, sometimes a bit wet behind the ears and stubborn as mules. Their love of money and the comfort it can bring may make them very materialistic in outlook. They are most suited to a practical career which brings with it few surprises and plenty of money. However, they have a strong artistic streak which can be expressed in work, hobbies and interests.

Some Taureans are quick and clever, highly amusing and quite outrageous in appearance, but underneath this crazy exterior is a background of true talent and very hard work. This type may be a touch arrogant. Other Taureans hate to be rushed or hassled, preferring to work quietly and thoroughly at their own pace. They take relationships very seriously and make safe and reliable partners. They may keep their worries to themselves but they are not usually liars or sexually untrustworthy.

Being so very sensual as well as patient, these people make excellent lovers. Their biggest downfall comes later in life when they have a tendency to plonk themselves down in front of the television night after night, tuning out the rest of the world. Another problem with some Taureans is their 'pet hate', which they'll harp on about at any given opportunity. Their virtues are common sense, loyalty, responsibility and a pleasant, non-hostile approach to others. Taureans are much brighter than anyone gives them credit, and it is hard to beat them in an argument because they usually know what they are talking about. If a Taurean is on your side, they make wonderful friends and comfortable and capable colleagues.

GEMINI
22nd May to 21st June

Geminis are often accused of being short on intellect and unable to stick to anyone or anything for long. In a nutshell, great fun at a party but totally unreliable. This is unfair: nobody works harder, is more reliable or capable than Geminis when they put their mind to a task, especially if there is a chance of making large sums of money! Unfortunately, they have a low boredom threshold and they can drift away from something or someone when it no longer interests them. They like to be busy, with plenty of variety in their lives and the opportunity to communicate with others. Their forte lies in the communications industry where they shamelessly pinch ideas and improve on them. Many Geminis are highly ambitious people who won't allow anything or anyone to stand in their way.

They are surprisingly constant in relationships, often marrying for life but, if it doesn't work out, they will walk out and put the experience behind them. Geminis need relationships and if one fails, they will soon start looking for the next. Faithfulness is another story, however, because the famous Gemini curiosity can lead to any number of adventures. Geminis educate their children well while neglecting to see whether they have a clean shirt. The house is full of books, videos, televisions, CDs, newspapers and magazines and there is a phone in every room as well as in the car, the loo and the Gemini lady's handbag.

LEO
24th July to 23rd August

Leos can be marvellous company or a complete pain in the neck. Under normal circumstances, they are warm-hearted, generous, sociable and popular but they can be very moody and irritable when under pressure or under the weather. Leos put their heart and soul into whatever they are doing and they can work like demons for a while. However, they cannot keep up the pace for long and they need to get away, zonk out on the sofa and take frequent holidays. These people always appear confident and they look like true winners, but their confidence can suddenly evaporate, leaving them unsure and unhappy with their efforts. They are extremely sensitive to hurt and they cannot take ridicule or even very much teasing.

Leos are proud. They have very high standards in all that they do and most have great integrity and honesty, but there are some who are complete and utter crooks. These people can stand on their dignity and be very snobbish. Their arrogance can become insufferable and they can take their powers of leadership into the realms of bossiness. They are convinced that they should be in charge and they can be very obstinate. Some Leos love the status and lifestyle which proclaims their successes. Many work in glamour professions such as the airline and entertainment industries. Others spend their day communing with computers and other high-tech gadgetry. In loving relationships, they are loyal but only while the magic lasts. If boredom sets in, they often start looking around for fresh fields. They are the most generous and loving of people and they need to play affectionately. Leos are kind, charming and they live life to the full.

VIRGO
24th August to 23rd September

Virgos are highly intelligent, interested in everything and everyone and happy to be busy with many jobs and hobbies. Many have some kind of specialized knowledge and most are good with their hands, but their nit-picking ways can infuriate colleagues. They find it hard to discuss their innermost feelings and this can make them hard to understand. In many ways, they are happier doing something practical than dealing with relationships. Virgos can also overdo the self-sacrificial bit and make themselves martyrs to other people's impractical lifestyles. They are willing to fit in with whatever is going on and can adjust to most things, but they mustn't neglect their own needs.

Although excellent communicators and wonderfully witty conversationalists, Virgos prefer to express their deepest feelings by actions rather than words.

Most avoid touching all but very close friends and family members and many find lovey-dovey behaviour embarrassing. They can be very highly sexed and may use this as a way of expressing love. Virgos are criticized a good deal as children and are often made to feel unwelcome in their childhood homes. In turn, they become very critical of others and they can use this in order to wound.

Many Virgos overcome inhibitions by taking up acting, music, cookery or sports. Acting is particularly common to this sign because it allows them to put aside their fears and take on the mantle of someone quite different. They are shy and slow to make friends but when they do accept someone, they are the loyalest, gentlest and kindest of companions. They are great company and have a wonderful sense of humour.

LIBRA
24th September to 23rd October

Librans have a deceptive appearance, looking soft but being tough and quite selfish underneath. Astrological tradition tells us that this sign is dedicated to marriage, but a high proportion of them prefer to remain single, particularly when a difficult relationship comes to an end. These people are great to tell secrets to because they never listen to anything properly and promptly forget whatever is said. The confusion between their desire to co-operate with others and the need for self-expression is even more evident when at work. The best job is one where they are a part of an organization but able to take responsibility and make their own decisions.

While some Librans are shy and lacking in confidence, others are strong and determined with definite leadership qualities. All need to find a job that entails dealing with others and which does not wear out their delicate nerves. All Librans are charming, sophisticated and diplomatic, but can be confusing for others. All have a strong sense of justice and fair play but most haven't the strength to take on a determinedly lame duck. They project an image which is attractive, chosen to represent their sense of status and refinement. Being inclined to experiment sexually, they are not the most faithful of partners and even goody-goody Librans are terrible flirts.

SCORPIO
24th October to 22nd November

Reliable, resourceful and enduring, Scorpios seem to be the strong men and women of the zodiac. But are they really? They can be nasty at times, dishing out what they see as the truth, no matter how unwelcome. Their own feelings are sensitive and they are easily hurt, but they won't show any hurt or weakness in themselves to others. When they are very low or unhappy, this turns inwards, attacking their immune systems and making them ill. However, they have great resilience and they bounce back time and again from the most awful ailments.

Nobody needs to love and be loved more than a Scorpio, but their partners must stand up to them because they will give anyone they don't respect a very hard time indeed. They are the most loyal and honest of companions, both in personal relationships and at work. One reason for this is their hatred of change or uncertainty. Scorpios enjoy being the power behind the throne with someone else occupying the hot seat. This way, they can quietly manipulate everyone, set one against another and get exactly what they want from the situation.

Scorpios' voices are their best feature, often low, well-modulated and cultured and these wonderful voices are used to the full in pleasant persuasion. These people are neither as highly sexed nor as difficult as most astrology books make out, but they do have their passions (even if these are not always for sex itself) and they like to be thought of as sexy. They love to shock and to appear slightly dangerous, but they also make kind-hearted and loyal friends, superb hosts and gentle people who are often very fond of animals. Great people when they are not being cruel, stingy or devious!

SAGITTARIUS
23rd November to 21st December

Sagittarians are great company because they are interested in everything and everyone. Broad-minded and lacking in prejudice, they are fascinated by even the strangest of people. With their optimism and humour, they are often the life and soul of the party, while they are in a good mood. They can become quite down-hearted, crabby and awkward on occasion, but not usually for long. They can be hurtful to others because they cannot resist speaking what they see as the truth, even if it causes embarrassment. However, their tactlessness is usually innocent and they have no desire to hurt.

Sagittarians need an unconventional lifestyle, preferably one which allows them to travel. They cannot be cooped up in a cramped environment and they need to meet new people and to explore a variety of ideas during their day's work. Money is not their god and they will work for a pittance if they feel inspired by the task. Their values are spiritual rather than material. Many are attracted to the spiritual side of life and may be interested in the Church, philosophy, astrology and other New Age subjects. Higher education and legal matters attract them because these subjects expand and explore intellectual boundaries. Long-lived relationships may not appeal because they need to feel free and unfettered, but they can do well with a self-sufficient and independent partner. Despite all this intellectualism and need for freedom, Sagittarians have a deep need to be cuddled and touched and they need to be supported emotionally.

CAPRICORN
22nd December to 20th January

Capricorns are patient, realistic and responsible and they take life seriously. They need security but they may find this difficult to achieve. Many live on a treadmill of work, simply to pay the bills and feed the kids. They will never shun family responsibilities, even caring for distant relatives if this becomes necessary. However, they can play the martyr while doing so. These people hate coarseness, they are easily embarrassed and they hate to annoy anyone. Capricorns believe fervently in keeping the peace in their families. This doesn't mean that they cannot stand up for themselves, indeed they know how to get their own way and they won't be bullied. They are adept at using charm to get around prickly people.

Capricorns are ambitious, hard-working, patient and status-conscious and they will work their way steadily towards the top in any organization. If they run their own businesses, they need a partner with more pizzazz to deal with sales and marketing for them while they keep an eye on the books. Their nit-picking habits can infuriate others and some have a tendency to 'know best' and not to listen. These people work at their hobbies with the same kind of dedication that they put into everything else. They are faithful and reliable in relationships and it takes a great deal to make them stray. If a relationship breaks up, they take a long time to get over it. They may marry very early or delay it until middle age when they are less shy. As an earth sign, Capricorns are highly sexed but they need to be in a relationship where they can relax and gain confidence. Their best attribute is their genuine kindness and their wonderfully dry, witty sense of humour.

AQUARIUS
21st January to 19th February

Clever, friendly, kind and humane, Aquarians are the easiest people to make friends with but probably the hardest to really know. They are often more comfortable with acquaintances than with those who are close to them. Being dutiful, they would never let a member of their family go without their basic requirements, but they can be strangely, even deliberately, blind to their underlying needs and real feelings. They are more comfortable with causes and their idealistic ideas than with the day-to-day routine of family life. Their homes may reflect this lack of interest by being rather messy, although there are other Aquarians who are almost clinically house proud.

Their opinions are formed early in life and are firmly fixed. Being patient with people, they make good teachers and are, themselves, always willing to learn something new. But are they willing to go out and earn a living? Some are, many are not. These people can be extremely eccentric in the way they dress or the way they live. They make a point of being 'different' and they can actually feel very unsettled and uneasy if made to conform, even outwardly. Their restless, sceptical minds mean that they need an alternative kind of lifestyle which stretches them mentally.

In relationships, they are surprisingly constant and faithful and they only stray when they know in their hearts that there is no longer anything to be gained from staying put. Aquarians are often very attached to the first real commitment in their lives and they can even remarry a previously divorced partner. Their sexuality fluctuates, perhaps peaking for some years then pushed aside while something else occupies their energies, then high again. Many Aquarians are extremely highly sexed and very clever and active in bed.

PISCES
20th February to 20th March

This idealistic, dreamy, kind and impractical sign needs a lot of understanding. They have a fractured personality which has so many sides and so many moods that they probably don't even understand themselves. Nobody is more kind, thoughtful and caring, but they have a tendency to drift away from people and responsibilities. When the going gets rough, they get going! Being creative, clever and resourceful, these people can achieve a great deal and really reach the top, but few of them do. Some Pisceans have a self-destruct button which they press before reaching their goal. Others do achieve success and the motivating force behind this essentially spiritual and mystical sign is often money. Many Pisceans feel insecure, most suffer some experience of poverty at some time in their early lives and they grow into adulthood determined that they will never feel that kind of uncertainty again.

Pisceans are at home in any kind of creative or caring career. Many can be found in teaching, nursing and the arts. Some find life hard and are often unhappy; many have to make tremendous sacrifices on behalf of others. This may be a pattern which repeats itself from childhood, where the message is that the Piscean's needs always come last. These people can be stubborn, awkward, selfish and quite nasty when a friendship or relationship goes sour. This is because, despite their basically kind and gentle personality, there is a side which needs to be in charge of any relationship. Pisceans make extremely faithful partners as long as the romance doesn't evaporate and their partners treat them well. Problems occur if they are mistreated or rejected, if they become bored or restless or if their alcohol intake climbs over the danger level. The Piscean lover is a sexual fantasist, so in this sphere of life anything can happen!

You and Yours

What is it like to bring up an Arien child? What kind of father does a Libran make? How does it feel to grow up with a Sagittarian mother? Whatever your own sign is, how do you appear to your parents and how do you behave towards your children?

THE CANCER FATHER

A true family man who will happily embrace even stepchildren as if they were his own. Letting go of the family when they grow up is another matter. Cancerian sulks, moodiness and bouts of childishness can confuse or frighten some children, while his changeable attitude to money can make them unsure of what they should ask for. This father enjoys domesticity and child-rearing and he may be happy to swap roles.

THE CANCER MOTHER

Cancerian women are excellent home makers and cheerful and reasonable mothers, as long as they have a part-time job or an interest outside the house. They instinctively know when a child is unhappy and can deal with it in a manner which is both efficient and loving. These women have a reputation for clinging but most are quite realistic when the time comes for their brood to leave the nest.

THE CANCER CHILD

These children are shy, cautious and slow to grow up. They may achieve little at school, 'disappearing' behind louder and more demanding classmates. They can be worriers who complain about every ache and pain or suffer from imaginary fears. They may take on the mother's role in the family, dictating to their sisters and brothers at times. Gentle and loving but moody and secretive, they need a lot of love and encouragement.

THE ARIES FATHER

Arien men take the duties of fatherhood very seriously. They read to their children, take them on educational trips and expose them to art and music from an early age. They can push their children too hard or tyrannize the sensitive ones. The Aries father wants his children not only to have what he didn't have but also to be what he isn't. He respects those children who are high achievers and who can stand up to him.

THE ARIES MOTHER

Arien women love their children dearly and will make amazing sacrifices for them, but don't expect them to give up their jobs or their outside interests for motherhood. Competitive herself, this mother wants her children to be the best and she may push them too hard. However, she is kind-hearted, affectionate and not likely to over-discipline them. She treats her offspring as adults and is well loved in return.

THE ARIES CHILD

Arien children are hard to ignore. Lively, noisy and demanding, they try to enjoy every moment of their childhood. Despite this, they lack confidence and need reassurance. Often clever but lacking in self-discipline, they need to be made to attend school each day and to do their homework. Active and competitive, these children excel in sports, dancing or learning to play a pop music instrument.

THE TAURUS FATHER

This man cares deeply for his children and wants the best for them, but doesn't expect the impossible. He may lay the law down and he can be unsympathetic to the attitudes and interests of a new generation. He may frighten young children by shouting at them. Being a responsible parent, he offers a secure family base but he may find it hard to let them go when they want to leave.

THE TAURUS MOTHER

These women make good mothers due to their highly domesticated nature. Some are real earth mothers, baking bread and making wonderful toys and games for their children. Sane and sensible but not highly imaginative, they do best with a child who has ordinary needs and they get confused by those who are 'special' in any way. Taurus mothers are very loving but they use reasonable discipline when necessary.

THE TAURUS CHILD

Taurean children can be surprisingly demanding. Their loud voices and stubborn natures can be irritating. Plump, sturdy and strong, some are shy and retiring, while others can bully weaker children. Artistic, sensual and often musical, these children can lose themselves in creative or beautiful hobbies. They need to be encouraged to share and express love and also to avoid too many sweet foods.

THE GEMINI FATHER

Gemini fathers are fairly laid back in their approach and, while they cope well with fatherhood, they can become bored with home life and try to escape from their duties. Some are so absorbed with work that they hardly see their offspring. At home, Gemini fathers will provide books, educational toys and as much computer equipment as the child can use, and they enjoy a family game of tennis.

THE GEMINI MOTHER

These mothers can be very pushy because they see education as the road to success. They encourage a child to pursue any interest and will sacrifice time and money for this. They usually have a job outside the home and may rely on other people to do some child-minding for them. Their children cannot always count on coming home to a balanced meal, but they can talk to their mothers on any subject.

THE GEMINI CHILD

These children needs a lot of reassurance because they often feel like square pegs in round holes. They either do very well at school and incur the wrath of less able children, or they fail dismally and have to make it up later in life. They learn to read early and some have excellent mechanical ability while others excel at sports. They get bored very easily and they can be extremely irritating.

THE LEO FATHER

These men can be wonderful fathers as long as they remember that children are not simply small and rather obstreperous adults. Leo fathers like to be involved with their children and encourage them to do well at school. They happily make sacrifices for their children and they truly want them to have the best, but they can be a bit too strict and they may demand too high a standard.

THE LEO MOTHER

Leo mothers are very caring and responsible but they cannot be satisfied with a life of pure domesticity, and need to combine motherhood with a job. These mothers don't fuss about minor details. They're prepared to put up with a certain amount of noise and disruption, but they can be irritable and they may demand too much of their children.

THE LEO CHILD

These children know almost from the day they are born that they are special. They are usually loved and wanted but they are also aware that a lot is expected from them. Leo children appear outgoing but they are surprisingly sensitive and easily hurt. They only seem to wake up to the need to study a day or so after they leave school, but they find a way to make a success of their lives.

THE VIRGO FATHER

These men may be embarrassed by open declarations of love and affection and find it hard to give cuddles and reassurance to small children. Yet they love their offspring dearly and will go to any lengths to see that they have the best possible education and outside activities. Virgoan men can become wrapped up in their work, forgetting to spend time relaxing and playing with their children.

THE VIRGO MOTHER

Virgoan women try hard to be good mothers because they probably had a poor childhood themselves. They love their children very much and want the best for them but they may be fussy about unnecessary details, such as dirt on the kitchen floor or the state of the children's school books. If they can keep their tensions and longings away from their children, they can be the most kindly and loving parents.

THE VIRGO CHILD

Virgoan children are practical and capable and can do very well at school, but they are not always happy. They don't always fit in and they may have difficulty making friends. They may be shy, modest and sensitive and they can find it hard to live up to their own impossibly high standards. Virgo children don't need harsh discipline, they want approval and will usually respond perfectly well to reasoned argument.

THE LIBRA FATHER

Libran men mean well, but they may not actually perform that well. They have no great desire to be fathers but welcome their children when they come along. They may slide out of the more irksome tasks by having an absorbing job or a series of equally absorbing hobbies which keep them occupied outside the home. These men do better with older children because they can talk to them.

THE LIBRA MOTHER

Libran mothers are pleasant and easy-going but some of them are more interested in their looks, their furnishings and their friends than their children. Others are very loving and kind but a bit too soft, which results in their children disrespecting them or walking all over them in later life. These mothers enjoy talking to their children and encouraging them to succeed.

THE LIBRA CHILD

These children are charming and attractive and they have no difficulty in getting on with people. They make just enough effort to get through school and only do the household jobs they cannot dodge. They may drive their parents mad with their demands for the latest gadget or gimmick. However, their common sense, sense of humour and reasonable attitude makes harsh discipline unnecessary.

THE SCORPIO FATHER

These fathers can be really awful or absolutely wonderful, and there aren't any half-measures. Good Scorpio men provide love and security because they stick closely to their homes and families and are unlikely to do a disappearing act. Difficult ones can be loud and tyrannical. These proud men want their children to be the best.

THE SCORPIO MOTHER

These mothers are either wonderful or not really maternal at all, although they try to do their best. If they take to child-rearing, they encourage their offspring educationally and in their hobbies. These mothers have no time for whiny or miserable children but they respect outgoing, talented and courageous ones, and can cope with a handful.

THE SCORPIO CHILD

Scorpio children are competitive, self-centred and unwilling to co-operate with brothers, sisters, teachers or anyone else when in an awkward mood. They can be deeply unreadable, living in a world of their own and filled with all kinds of strange angry feelings. At other times, they can be delightfully caring companions. They love animals, sports, children's organizations and group activities.

THE SAGITTARIUS FATHER

Sagittarian fathers will give their children all the education they can stand. They happily provide books, equipment and take their offspring out to see anything interesting. They may not always be available to their offspring, but they make up for it by surprising their families with tickets for sporting events or by bringing home a pet for the children. These men are cheerful and childlike themselves.

THE SAGITTARIUS MOTHER

This mother is kind, easy-going and pleasant. She may be very ordinary with suburban standards or she may be unbelievably eccentric, forcing the family to take up strange diets and filling the house with weird and wonderful people. Some opt out of child-rearing by finding childminders while others take on other people's children and a host of animals in addition to their own.

THE SAGITTARIUS CHILD

Sagittarian children love animals and the outdoor life but they are just as interested in sitting around and watching the telly as the next child. These children have plenty of friends whom they rush out and visit at every opportunity. Happy and optimistic but highly independent, they cannot be pushed in any direction. Many leave home in late their teens in order to travel.

THE CAPRICORN FATHER

These are true family men who cope with housework and child-rearing but they are sometimes too involved in work to spend much time at home. Dutiful and caring, these men are unlikely to run off with a bimbo or to leave their family wanting. However, they can be stuffy or out of touch with the younger generation. They encourage their children to do well and to behave properly.

THE CAPRICORN MOTHER

Capricorn women make good mothers but they may be inclined to fuss. Being ambitious, they want their children to do well and they teach them to respect teachers, youth leaders and so on. These mothers usually find work outside the home in order to supplement the family income. They are very loving but they can be too keen on discipline and the careful management of pocket money.

THE CAPRICORN CHILD

Capricorn children are little adults from the day they are born. They don't need much discipline or encouragement to do well at school. Modest and well behaved, they are almost too good to be true. However, they suffer badly with their nerves and can be prone to ailments such as asthma. They need to be taught to let go, have fun and enjoy their childhood. Some are too selfish or ambitious to make friends.

THE AQUARIAN FATHER

Some Aquarian men have no great desire to be fathers but they make a reasonable job of it when they have to. They cope best when their children are reasonable and intelligent but, if they are not, they tune out and ignore them. Some Aquarians will spend hours inventing games and toys for their children while all of them value education and try to push their children.

THE AQUARIAN MOTHER

Some of these mothers are too busy putting the world to rights to see what is going on in their own family. However, they are kind, reasonable and keen on education. They may be busy outside the house but they often take their children along with them. They are not fussy homemakers, and are happy to have all the neighbourhood kids in the house. They respect a child's dignity.

THE AQUARIAN CHILD

These children may be demanding when very young but they become much more reasonable when at school. They are easily bored and need outside interests. They have many friends and may spend more time in other people's homes than in their own. Very stubborn and determined, they make it quite clear from an early age that they intend to do things their own way. These children suffer from nerves.

THE PISCES FATHER

Piscean men fall into one of two categories. Some are kind and gentle, happy to take their children on outings and to introduce them to art, culture, music or sport. Others are disorganized and unpredictable. The kindly fathers don't always push their children. They encourage their kids to have friends and a pet or two.

THE PISCES MOTHER

Piscean mothers may be lax and absent-minded but they love their children and are usually loved in return. Many are too disorganized to run a perfect household so meals, laundry, etc. can be hit and miss, but their children prosper despite this, although many learn to reverse the mother/child roles. These mothers teach their offspring to appreciate animals and the environment.

THE PISCES CHILD

These sensitive children may find life difficult and they can get lost among stronger, more demanding brothers and sisters. They may drive their parents batty with their dreamy attitude and they can make a fuss over nothing. They need a secure and loving home with parents who shield them from harsh reality while encouraging them to develop their imaginative and psychic abilities.

Your Rising Sign

WHAT IS A RISING SIGN?

Your rising sign is the sign of the zodiac which was climbing up over the eastern horizon the moment you were born. This is not the same as your Sun sign; your Sun sign depends upon your date of birth, but your rising sign depends upon the time of day that you were born, combined with your date and place of birth.

The rising sign modifies your Sun sign character quite considerably, so when you have worked out which is your rising sign, read pages 39–40 to see how it modifies your Sun sign. Then take a deeper look by going back to 'All the Other Sun Signs' on page 21 and read the relevant Sun sign material there to discover more about your ascendant (rising sign) nature.

One final point is that the sign that is opposite your rising sign (or 'ascendant') is known as your 'descendant'. This shows what you want from other people, and it may give a clue as to your choice of friends, colleagues and lovers (see pages 41–3). So once you have found your rising sign and read the character interpretation, check out the character reading for your descendant to see what you are looking for in others.

How to Begin

Read through this section while following the example below. Even if you only have a vague idea of your birth time, you won't find this method difficult; just go for a rough time of birth and then read the Sun sign information for that sign to see if it fits your personality. If you seem to be more like the sign that comes before or after it, then it is likely that you were born a little earlier or later than your assumed time of birth. Don't forget to deduct an hour for summertime births.

1. Look at the illustration top right. You will notice that it has the time of day arranged around the outer circle. It looks a bit like a clock face, but it is different because it shows the whole 24-hour day in two-hour blocks.

2. Write the astrological symbol that represents the Sun (a circle with a dot in the middle) in the segment that corresponds to your time of birth. (If you were born during Daylight Saving or British Summer Time, deduct one hour from your birth time.) Our example shows someone who was born between 2 a.m. and 4 a.m.

3. Now write the name of your sign or the symbol for your sign on the line which is at the end of the block of time that your Sun falls into. Our example shows a person who was born between 2 a.m. and 4 a.m. under the sign of Pisces.

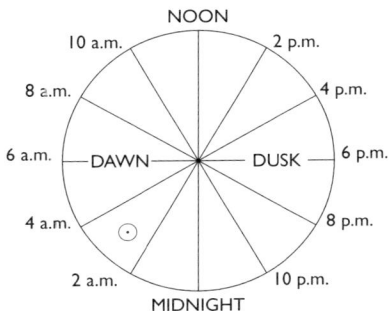

4. Either write in the names of the zodiac signs or use the symbols in their correct order (see the key below) around the chart in an anti-clockwise direction, starting from the line which is at the start of the block of time that your sun falls into.

5. The sign that appears on the left-hand side of the wheel at the 'Dawn' line is your rising sign, or ascendant. The example shows a person born with the Sun in Pisces and with Aquarius rising. Incidentally, the example chart also shows Leo, which falls on the 'Dusk' line, in the descendant. You will always find the ascendant sign on the 'Dawn' line and the descendant sign on the 'Dusk' line.

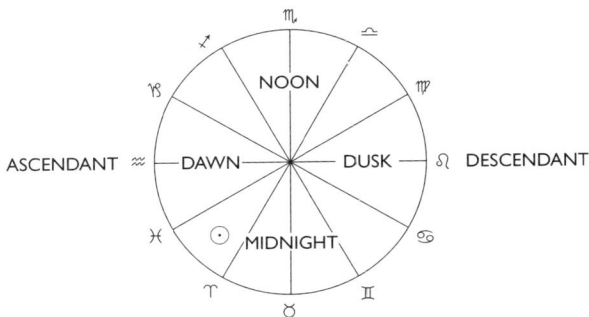

	Aries		Cancer		Libra		Capricorn
	Taurus		Leo		Scorpio		Aquarius
	Gemini		Virgo		Sagittarius		Pisces

Here is another example for you to run through, just to make sure that you have grasped the idea correctly. This example is for a more awkward time of birth, being exactly on the line between two different blocks of time. This example is for a person with a Capricorn Sun sign who was born at 10 a.m.

1. The Sun is placed exactly on the 10 a.m. line.

2. The sign of Capricorn is placed on the 10 a.m. line.

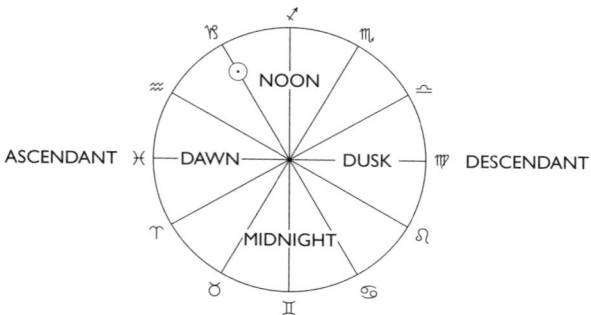

3. All the other signs are placed in astrological order (anti-clockwise) around the chart.

4. This person has the Sun in Capricorn and Pisces rising, and therefore with Virgo on the descendant.

Using the Rising Sign Finder

Please bear in mind that this method is approximate. If you want to be really sure of your rising sign, you should contact an astrologer. However, this system will work with reasonable accuracy wherever you were born, although it would be worth checking out the Sun and ascendant combination in the following pages. You should also read the Sun sign character readings on pages 21–8 for the signs both before and after the rising sign you think is yours. This is especially important for those of you whose ascendant is right at the beginning or the end of the zodiac sign. Rising signs are such an obvious part of one's personality that one quick glance will show you which one belongs to you.

Can Your Rising Sign Tell You More about Your Future?

When it comes to tracking events, the rising sign is equal in importance to the Sun sign. So, if you want a more accurate forecast when reading newspapers or magazines, you should read the horoscope for your rising sign as well as your Sun sign. In the case of books such as this, you should really treat yourself to two: one to correspond with your rising sign, and another for your usual Sun sign, and read both each day!

How Your Rising Sign Modifies Your Sun Sign

CANCER WITH ARIES RISING Your tough outer manner hides a soft inside. You care for the underdog but you have no patience with people who won't help themselves.

CANCER WITH TAURUS RISING You could be very keen on art or music and also a very creative cook. You need money in the bank and a loving family around you.

CANCER WITH GEMINI RISING Your go-getting nature gives you more outer confidence than the average Cancerian. You could study history or write about it for a living.

CANCER WITH CANCER RISING This is the purest form of the sign of

Cancer, so this combination is very strong. You are caring, home-loving and quite money-minded. Your moods fluctuate, especially if you were born after dawn. You will be more fiery, self-centred and outgoing if born before dawn.

CANCER WITH LEO RISING You are more outgoing than the average Cancerian, but you also have a desire to explore your inner life and to find the true meaning of things.

CANCER WITH VIRGO RISING The medical world may appeal to you. You could be interested in health and healing, and you also seek to help those who are weak or needy.

CANCER WITH LIBRA RISING This is quite a powerful combination which makes for a successful person with a very charming nature. You would thoroughly enjoy family life, as long as you could have a career too.

CANCER WITH SCORPIO RISING You are extremely intuitive and your feelings are sensitive and easily hurt. However, you can be tough and determined when you need to be.

CANCER WITH SAGITTARIUS RISING Your career is important to you but home is where your heart is. You need a deeply committed personal relationship but you also need your freedom.

CANCER WITH CAPRICORN RISING Your parents are a strong influence on you and you may follow them into the family business. You have a strong need for personal and financial security.

CANCER WITH AQUARIUS RISING Your idealistic streak could lead you to work for needy people, for animals or as a teacher. You guard your home life and keep it private.

CANCER WITH PISCES RISING You are extremely sensitive, and also probably psychic. Religion or mysticism may interest you, and your family means a lot to you.

Cancer in Love

YOU NEED:

FAMILY LIFE You need a home base and a close and loving family. You will even take on a step-family and look after them if necessary, because you have a caring nature and a lot of love to give.

SENSITIVITY Your confidence is not always all that great so you don't need a partner who puts you down all the time. A strong partner is great but he or she must also have a great deal of consideration for your feelings.

COMPANIONSHIP You may be strongly sexual or not really bothered about it but, either way, you need friendship, companionship and conversation from your lover. You may even choose someone whom you can work with.

YOU GIVE:

SUPPORT Your lover can count on your support in anything that he or she wants to do, as long as it is sensible and likely to lead somewhere. You will even help out on a really crazy scheme if it looks like being fun.

ATTENTION You are good listener with the patience to sit still and really hear what your partner has to say. It may hurt you to hear the truth at times but you will listen and try to understand his or her point of view.

ROMANCE You are good about birthdays and anniversaries and you love to celebrate these with due ceremony. You don't take a partner for granted but like to show your love by buying small gifts from time to time.

WHAT YOU CAN EXPECT FROM THE OTHER ZODIAC SIGNS:

ARIES *Truth, honesty, playfulness.* You can expect an open and honest relationship with no hidden agendas. Your Arien lover will be a bit childish at times, however.

TAURUS *Security, stability, comfort.* The Taurean will stand by you and try to improve your financial position. Taureans create beautiful homes and gardens for their partners.

GEMINI *Stimulation, encouragement, variety.* This lover will never bore you; Geminis give encouragement and are always ready for an outing.

LEO *Affection, fun, loyalty.* Leo lovers are very steadfast and they would avenge anyone who hurt one of their family. They enjoy romping and playing affectionate love games.

VIRGO *Clear thinking, kindness, humour.* Virgoans make intelligent and amusing partners. They can be critical but are never unkind. They take their responsibility towards you seriously.

LIBRA *Fair-play, sensuality, advice.* Librans will listen to your problems and give balanced and sensible advice. They are wonderfully inventive, and are affectionate lovers too.

SCORPIO *Truth, passion, loyalty.* Scorpios will take your interests as seriously as they do their own. They will stick by you when the going gets tough and they wonít flannel you.

SAGITTARIUS *Honesty, fun, novelty.* These lovers will effortlessly keep up with whatever pace you set. They seek the truth and they donít keep their feelings hidden.

CAPRICORN *Companionship, common sense, laughter.* Capricorns enjoy doing things together and they won't leave you in the lurch when the going gets tough. They can make you laugh too.

AQUARIUS *Stimulation, friendship, sexuality.* Aquarians are friends as well as lovers. They are great fun because you never know what they are going to do next, in or out of bed.

PISCES *Sympathy, support, love.* These romantic lovers never let you down. They can take you with them into their personal fantasy world and they are always ready for a laugh.

WHICH SIGN ARE YOU COMPATIBLE WITH?

CANCER/ARIES
Shared family and business interests, can be good match.

CANCER/TAURUS
Much in common, especially travel and family life.

CANCER/GEMINI
Cancer mothers Gemini and Gemini likes being mothered.

CANCER/CANCER
Either complete harmony or too similar for comfort.

CANCER/LEO
Oddly enough, this works well because both need stability.

CANCER/VIRGO
This could work because both are caring and family-minded.

CANCER/LIBRA
Either excellent or disastrous depending.

CANCER/SCORPIO
Can work as long as Scorpio is not too domineering.

CANCER/SAGITTARIUS
Very little in common, Cancer
clings, Sagittarius needs freedom.

CANCER/AQUARIUS
These two find it hard to
understand each other.

CANCER/CAPRICORN
Excellent combination, for love or
business.

CANCER/PISCES
Could work well, both intuitive and
sensitive.

Your Prospects for 1999

LOVE

At long last, this is your year! Over the past goodness knows how long, you
have watched others find love while you have either been struggling along in
a poor relationship or trying to get things off the ground that simply wouldn't
work for you. By now you are probably convinced that there is something
terribly wrong with you. Well, there isn't! However, even this year, nothing
may become as settled and comfortable as you would like and you may have
to settle for passion, romance and excitement instead for a while. It is
possible that a love affair that may seem badly starred during the first half of
the year comes right for you during the second half. Another possibility is
that you have a classic holiday romance or short fling during the first half of
the year and then meet someone much more settled and sensible later on.
Either way, you will end the year feeling much happier about your love
situation. The muddle that has surrounded settled relationships and transient
ones alike will leave you this year and by the end of the year you will know
exactly where you are going and that it is all worthwhile. Do take care with
financial arrangements with lovers though, as these will be a bit up and down
during this year. If your partner is a muddler, try to sort financial matters out
yourself rather than to allow them to drift into a mess.

MONEY AND WORK

As long as you handle your finances yourself, there should be no real problem
this year but if you get into any kind of joint venture or group activity with
others, there could be unexpected gains and losses. A series of eclipses make
this even more obvious as there could be explosions in the financial area of
your life when these occur. The dates of these events are the 31st of January,
the 16th of February, the 28th of July and the 11th of August. You could gain

substantially as a result of buying or selling property or of some kind of property dealings this year. Although your own judgement will generally be pretty good, you will have to guard against financial muddles during July and August when a couple of planets turn retrograde in the money area of your sign. As far as jobs and work is concerned anything that involves some form of teaching and also of helping or guiding others would be successful for you this year. Whatever kind of job you do, or even if you don't work at all, you will make your greatest efforts and your largest achievements during September and October this year, and Jupiter at the top of your chart suggests that there is a fair chance that you will achieve most of your ambitions now.

HEALTH

You will certainly be more conscious of the need to keep fit and you will be very active in trying to bring this about for yourself and for others. Oddly enough, there doesn't seem to be any health problem around that makes you focus on well-being, it just seems to be something that starts to interest you now. This may be no more than a decision to lose weight and to take some extra exercise in order to look better. The only time that the planets are even mildly against you healthwise will be during the first week of August.

FAMILY AND HOME

Family matters will be rather interesting this year and for the most part, rather lucky. It may have been hard for you to find or make the kind of home you really want over the past two years but those problems will start to fade during the first couple of months of the year, fading away completely after March. You may recently have moved house or you may be in the middle of renovating a property. Alternatively, you may be on the point of doing so. If so, May and June could be difficult times when things go wrong but both before and after that time, property matters will be rather exciting. There is no real reason for you to worry about family members and children in particular will have a generally good year.

LUCK

Luck from gambles and speculation could well pay pretty off for you this year, especially during the second half of the year, albeit with the exception of most of October and November which are not terribly lucky times for you. Most of your luck will come in the form of achievement rather than as windfalls this year, and if you have any personal or career ambitions, these should be easy to achieve.

The Aspects and their Astrological Meanings

CONJUNCT	This shows important events which are usually, but not always, good.
SEXTILE	Good, particularly for work and mental activity.
SQUARE	Difficult, challenging.
TRINE	Great for romance, family life and creativity.
OPPOSITE	Awkward, depressing, challenging.
INTO	This shows when a particular planet enters a new sign of the zodiac, thus setting off a new phase or a new set of circumstances.
DIRECT	When a planet resumes normal direct motion.
RETROGRADE	When a planet apparently begins to go backwards.
VOID	When the Moon makes no aspect to any planet.

September at a Glance

LOVE	❤	❤		
WORK	★	★		
MONEY	£	£	£	£
HEALTH	✚	✚	✚	
LUCK	U	U	U	

TUESDAY, 1ST SEPTEMBER
Moon trine Saturn

A very practical plan will be presented by your partner or close friend. There may be a lot of work involved, yet this idea is splendid and deserves serious attention.

WEDNESDAY, 2ND SEPTEMBER
Void Moon

The term 'void of course' means that neither the Moon nor any of the other planets are making any important aspects during the course of their travels. When this kind of day occurs, the best thing to do is keep to routine tasks and leave your inspired ideas for a more auspicious time.

THURSDAY, 3RD SEPTEMBER
Moon conjunct Neptune

You'll be in a deeply sensitive, not to say impressionable, mood for much of the day. Romantically, this is good news since you'll be in tune with someone special. However, don't allow yourself to be persuaded into a course of action that doesn't feel right.

FRIDAY, 4TH SEPTEMBER
Mars opposite Uranus

The financial outlook doesn't look too promising today. Mars and Uranus are at odds, sending your cash flow into a dramatic slide! Some equally powerful action is required to redress the balance. At least you will have the courage and tenacity to tackle it.

CANCER

SATURDAY, 5TH SEPTEMBER
Moon opposite Venus

Don't be taken in by attractive offers or apparent bargains today because you'll find that for every cent saved you'll pay a dollar in repair bills. Shoddy goods and glib promises are the main dangers, as is attractive packaging. Equally, any desire to spend beyond your means should be curbed immediately.

SUNDAY, 6TH SEPTEMBER
Full Moon eclipse

There is a definite 'let's get away from it all' feeling about your stars. You may book a holiday now, and the best arrangement would be to rent a place where the family can join you if they so desire. Think about your cultural background and consider your prejudices, because you could be missing out by excluding friends from diverse backgrounds.

MONDAY, 7TH SEPTEMBER
Moon sextile Neptune

It's a great day to plan an outing with a loved one. A break away from routine will do you both the world of good, so get down to the travel agency and book a holiday!

TUESDAY, 8TH SEPTEMBER
Mercury into Virgo

Mercury enters your Solar house of communications, travel and education from today so this is the start of a period of chat, information and gossip. Close friends and neighbours may have concerns about the environment that you'd be wise to listen to. Of course you have a few salient points to add yourself, so don't be afraid to make your views known. Anything connected to journeys and schooling should go well.

WEDNESDAY, 9TH SEPTEMBER
Mercury trine Saturn

There's easy communication amongst old friends today. Your social life will be full and very satisfying as you reacquaint yourself with people you may not have seen in ages. Having said this, flippant conversation is not really on the agenda. Everyone concerned will be more interested in serious topics.

THURSDAY, 10TH SEPTEMBER
Venus trine Saturn

A much-needed chat with an older friend will clarify your feelings today. If you've been torn between duty and pleasure you'll find that now there's time for both. A sense of commitment is evident in all your relationships, platonic or romantic.

FRIDAY, 11TH SEPTEMBER
Mercury conjunct Venus

Communication will be the name of the game today, so get on the phone, write all those letters and be ready to run errands for yourself and others. You need to sort out your diary and clear the decks for the future, as you seem destined for a period of hard work and a packed social life. Any feelings of fatigue and malaise will slip away and your energies will be restored.

SATURDAY, 12TH SEPTEMBER
Moon sextile Mars

Your mood is quite ethereal today, but those around you may have much more down-to-earth ideas. Nevertheless, if you fancy popping into your local church or temple for a little spiritual nourishment, then feel free to do so.

SUNDAY, 13TH SEPTEMBER
Moon square Jupiter

You're delving into your own private world again today. Your imagination is very powerful and you'll be seeing things not as they are, but as you'd like them to be. You may review your life and realize how much you have learned as well as gained in the material sense.

MONDAY, 14TH SEPTEMBER
Moon sextile Venus

You're about to take the social scene by storm! You're a maestro of dazzling wit and repartee, and your popularity is guaranteed as you eloquently hold forth on any subject under the sun. A lot of laughs and entertaining conversations are in store.

TUESDAY, 15TH SEPTEMBER
Moon sextile Sun

A reunion with a brother, sister, or other relative of your own age will be marvellous today. You'll get the chance to have a long talk and catch up on all the gossip.

WEDNESDAY, 16TH SEPTEMBER
Sun opposite Jupiter

Although you are quite forward-looking and confident today, you may not receive the support you expect from your family. In fact, you could feel somewhat let down by their negative attitudes to your aspirations and ideas. Don't let this apparent coldness deceive you – your relations are preoccupied with their own concerns. Concentrate on inner strength; you've got plenty of it.

THURSDAY, 17TH SEPTEMBER
Moon conjunct Mars

Your mood is excitable, possibly with good reason. You have plenty to look forward to at the moment, and whether good things come your way sooner or later is immaterial. Your energy levels are high and you're feeling happy and confident.

FRIDAY, 18TH SEPTEMBER
Moon trine Saturn

This is an excellent time to embark on something unusual, off-beat or educational, with long-term projects being better starred than short-term ones. If you are in contact with parents or parental figures, then it's a good idea to get in touch today, because you should hear something from them or about them that pleases you greatly.

SATURDAY, 19TH SEPTEMBER
Mercury opposite Jupiter

Today the opposition between Mercury and Jupiter shows that you aren't really prepared for stubbornness. You can't win an argument now – those around you will only dig in their heels, so try to avoid confrontation.

SUNDAY, 20TH SEPTEMBER
New Moon

The New Moon shows a change in your way of thinking. In many ways you'll know that it's time to move on. Perhaps you'll find yourself in different company, in a new home or among a new circle of friends in the near future. Your opinions are likely to change as you become influenced by more stimulating people. Perhaps you'll consider taking up an educational course of some kind.

MONDAY, 21ST SEPTEMBER
Moon sextile Pluto

Everything in the garden is rather rosy today. Whether you invite your mother-in-law over to dinner, or try the equally dangerous sport of bungee jumping, today should be great fun! Your mood is warm and sexy but your desires seem to be confined to your partner and your home, which means that fanciable person who is trying to catch your eye won't stand a chance.

TUESDAY, 22ND SEPTEMBER
Sun trine Neptune

Your are full of good ideas and you want to share them with your friends. You, too, could learn something – if you manage to shut up long enough to listen! This should be an enjoyable time with plenty of gossip and information coming your way. Of course not all of it holds water, but it'll be fun all the same.

WEDNESDAY, 23RD SEPTEMBER
Sun into Libra

The Sun moves into your Solar area of family and domestic issues for the next month. These spheres of life will now become very important to you. If you have neglected your home or failed to pay the right amount of attention to your family, this is the time to put things right.

THURSDAY, 24TH SEPTEMBER
Mercury into Libra

Your life is going to be extremely busy for a while now, and there will be little time to sit around and rest. You will have more to do with friends, relatives, colleagues and neighbours than is usual and you could be busy sorting out minor domestic and work problems with workmen and women of various kinds. You may also spend time and money sorting out a vehicle.

FRIDAY, 25TH SEPTEMBER
Sun conjunct Mercury

A good chat with a relative could open up possibilities and reveal old secrets today. The Sun meets up with Mercury in your Solar house of heritage and family issues, so you'll take a great deal of pleasure in the company of those who are close to you. This should also be a time to look to the future. Perhaps moving home could be considered now.

SATURDAY, 26TH SEPTEMBER
Moon conjunct Pluto

There is a feeling that hidden factors are coming out of the woodwork at your workplace. Someone may have been saying or doing something behind your back, and today their activities are beginning to come to light. Although these power games may have nothing to do with you, they'll still have the ability to irritate.

SUNDAY, 27TH SEPTEMBER
Mercury sextile Pluto

Good news on the job front will boost your self-confidence and rub off on your home life. You'll be eager to tell your nearest and dearest all about the developments that have got you so excited. Family members too will have good news to share.

MONDAY, 28TH SEPTEMBER
Moon trine Saturn

A suggestion made by your spouse or indeed a close friend should be heeded today. This comment will have a wealth of common sense in it, and is not one you can afford to ignore.

TUESDAY, 29TH SEPTEMBER
Sun sextile Pluto

You could decide to break the habits of a lifetime today, and you'll find there's no better time to do so! Many will consider giving up smoking, taking up a more healthy diet and generally looking after yourself more – and there's nothing wrong with any of that!

WEDNESDAY, 30TH SEPTEMBER
Venus into Libra

This is a good time to spend in and around your home. You may want to get the garden into shape or do some kind of farming work on your land. The atmosphere around you should be harmonious and happy, and you should be pleased with your achievements. If you have been at odds with any of your relatives, kiss and make up today.

October at a Glance

LOVE	♥			
WORK	★	★	★	
MONEY	£			
HEALTH	✪	✪	✪	✪
LUCK	U			

CANCER

THURSDAY, 1ST OCTOBER
Sun trine Uranus

This could be your lucky day! Whatever happens, you are in for a few pleasant surprises. You may be asked to make a start on a new and exciting project which may involve you in a lucrative or a pleasantly enjoyable joint venture. You may discover that a long-lost uncle has left you a fortune or you may be blessed with a wonderfully useful idea. A day to remember.

FRIDAY, 2ND OCTOBER
Moon opposite Mars

Hang on to your cash and hang on to your wallet! Don't leave money or credit cards lying around where light-fingered people can get their hands on them. It's also worth staying away from the shops in order to avoid spending on unwanted or overpriced items.

SATURDAY, 3RD OCTOBER
Moon square Pluto

You may find that some kind of public or political event gets in the way of your plans today. Maybe the roads will be jammed with traffic due to a sports fixture, or perhaps schools will be closed due to industrial action. Be patient!

SUNDAY, 4TH OCTOBER
Moon conjunct Jupiter

This is really a day for optimism and happiness as the Moon contacts Jupiter. All your hopes are lifted by this harmonious combination. Of course you are now in a lucky period, but don't rely on it too much. You've got to complement good fortune with some efforts of your own.

MONDAY, 5TH OCTOBER
Venus sextile Pluto

Deep feelings are roused today as an old family situation arises. This is not such a bad thing, since you have now learned how to deal with it by referring to past experience. Aside from that, the aspect of Venus to Pluto should be good news for your love life.

TUESDAY, 6TH OCTOBER
Full Moon

The career-orientated Full Moon urges you to reassess your aims and ambitions today. You've achieved many of the things you set out to do so many years ago, but you may not have noticed. It's time you opened your eyes to new possibilities at work as maybe you've gone as far as you can in one particular direction and could do with a change.

WEDNESDAY, 7TH OCTOBER
Mars into Virgo

Mars moves into your Solar house of communications today, so you'll be rather forthright for a while. Amicable disagreements could easily turn into shouting matches because you won't have the patience to tolerate a contrary point of view. On the other hand, this is quite a good time to make a stand on an important principle. Determination is your forte now.

THURSDAY, 8TH OCTOBER
Moon sextile Jupiter

There's no doubt that you're determined to improve your position as far as professional achievement and standing is concerned, but you may feel that some improvement of the mind is needed too. Perhaps an educational course at an evening class would appeal now? Remember, focus your energy now and you'll be amply rewarded with success.

FRIDAY, 9TH OCTOBER
Moon trine Uranus

Something will surprise you today and, fortunately this surprise will be welcome. There may be great news for a friend, or it may be that a friend is responsible for bringing great news to you. Any dealings that you have with joint finances or working partnerships will go well now.

SATURDAY, 10TH OCTOBER
Mars trine Saturn

Your energy levels are certainly high today. You'll leave everyone else standing as you dash about doing a million and one things, and all to a good end. You won't be content until you have achieved everything to your satisfaction. Try not to push yourself too hard, though.

SUNDAY, 11TH OCTOBER
Neptune direct

Today, that distant and very mysterious planet, Neptune, turns to direct motion. This will bring an end to any misunderstandings concerning partnerships. You get your personal relationships on a better footing and working associations will be easier to handle. You will have more idea of what you want from these relationships, and you'll be able to tell others what you need from them.

CANCER

MONDAY, 12TH OCTOBER
Mercury into Scorpio

Over the next two or three weeks something will capture your attention and keep you amused. You may take an interest in intellectual games such as bridge, chess or other board games. You may get your mind into gear by doing quizzes or crosswords. There is also a fair chance that you could win something through a competition of some kind. Read ahead to find the best days for lucky chances.

TUESDAY, 13TH OCTOBER
Moon square Mercury

Just because you are happy and finding life rather exciting, you shouldn't neglect all those boring details that have to be dealt with. Try to keep some part of your mind on the job and don't allow your credit cards to have a life of their own! Keep your feet on the ground to avoid future problems.

WEDNESDAY, 14TH OCTOBER
Mercury sextile Mars

There's no doubt that you're feeling particularly brave today. Decide what you want to accomplish early and then go out and do it! Nothing can stop you as long as you believe in yourself. You may be reasonably argumentative, but that's only because you won't tolerate any obstacles.

THURSDAY, 15TH OCTOBER
Moon trine Saturn

Those of you who, through no fault of your own, abandoned education at an early age, or did badly at school, may wish to improve your knowledge and qualifications. Although the Lunar aspect to Saturn makes you painfully aware of your deficiencies, you shouldn't feel that you are unintelligent! There's always a chance to make good a bad situation. Do something practical about furthering your academic career now.

FRIDAY, 16TH OCTOBER
Moon square Pluto

You could be harbouring some hidden resentments at the moment. Perhaps you feel that a colleague isn't pulling his weight, or that you have too much on your plate to cope with. Keeping these feelings hidden won't solve the problem, so tactfully suggest a little more effort on the part of your co-worker.

CANCER

SATURDAY, 17TH OCTOBER
Mercury square Uranus

Don't be alarmed by anything you hear today! Gossip is likely to be inaccurate or a downright lie! There could be a hidden motive behind this attempt to give you the jitters. Think carefully before you react.

SUNDAY, 18TH OCTOBER
Uranus direct

Uranus turns to direct motion today, bringing a difficult phase to an end. The improvements will come in connection with deep and committed relationships of one kind or another, and this change of direction for Uranus will help greatly. If personal relationships have been hampered by mystery, lies or interference, the situation is about to improve dramatically.

MONDAY, 19TH OCTOBER
Mars square Pluto

You could feel rather out of sorts today as the negative Mars-Pluto aspect affects your health area. The cause of this could be some ill-feeling at work which has increased your stress levels. An outburst of temper won't do your blood pressure much good, so try to restrain yourself.

TUESDAY, 20TH OCTOBER
New Moon

The New Moon in the area of domestic life and heritage shows that memories of childhood become very important now. Things learned then may now be questioned as you look back and try to relate happenings in early life to events today. You must admit that the world has changed immeasurably, so some concepts are rather dated. On the other hand, firm values passed down to you are as valid now as they ever were. Of course, you have to work out the difference for yourself.

WEDNESDAY, 21ST OCTOBER
Moon square Uranus

There will be tension in the family today and it's likely that you'll get stuck in the middle of it. Your partner may fall out with one of your parents or a parent may disagree with someone else in the family. Older people, those who are in positions of authority and parental figures in general could be feeling tense and tetchy.

THURSDAY, 22ND OCTOBER
Sun square Neptune

You may tend to look at your family, your lover and your close associates through rose-tinted spectacles today, thinking that they are wonderful when they're really quite ordinary! You seem to be exceptionally willing to help your family now, either in practical ways or by handing over large sums of money. Make sure that this craziness doesn't go on for too long!

FRIDAY, 23RD OCTOBER
Sun into Scorpio

The Sun's movement into your fifth Solar house shows that you've had enough of being dutiful and working your fingers to the bone. You now desperately need some fun, and it won't do you any harm at all to please yourself for the next month or so. Think of something you really enjoy and go for it. Artistic ventures of all kinds, whether dramatic, poetic, literary or just a love of a good film should be indulged to the full ... you'll feel far better for it.

SATURDAY, 24TH OCTOBER
Venus into Scorpio

The two themes that are likely to be important in the short-term future are those of children and having a good time. We hope that these two are compatible.

SUNDAY, 25TH OCTOBER
Saturn into Pisces retrograde

Saturn's return to your house of philosophy and travel puts the spanner in the works as far as distant journeys go. Delays, unforeseen problems and red tape all combine to irritate you. You may also lack concentration and be too mean for your own good.

MONDAY, 26TH OCTOBER
Sun conjunct Venus

This cannot fail to be a highly romantic day as the Sun and Venus combine in such a flirtatious area of your chart. All relationships flourish under such a beneficial influence, so show affection and receive warmth and love from those around you.

TUESDAY, 27TH OCTOBER
Moon sextile Mercury

It's a day of group effort for you and your family. Discourage any overly independent attitudes now, for a sense of togetherness prevails in your domestic environment. It may be that you can help out a relative who is in need of advice, or maybe you need some familial support yourself.

WEDNESDAY, 28TH OCTOBER
Moon square Sun

You're in the mood for fun and adventure, but those close to home won't appreciate your apparently selfish actions. A money worry may emerge today which will do little to encourage domestic harmony. Very little can be resolved, so wait until this stellar influence passes.

THURSDAY, 29TH OCTOBER
Saturn square Neptune

Lofty values have no place in today's rather disappointing stars. You may feel you have been let down by colleagues who do not share your ideals. Perhaps you're feeling moody and distrustful … however, there is probably a good reason for this.

FRIDAY, 30TH OCTOBER
Moon sextile Saturn

Someone may do or say something today that comes as a revelation. You may begin to question your beliefs or, alternatively, add this new information to your own stock of ideas. The chances are that the person who enlightens you in this way is either a good bit older than you are or is in a position of authority.

SATURDAY, 31ST OCTOBER
Moon conjunct Jupiter

You'll be fired with enthusiasm today and filled with ambitious thoughts. You'll have a strong desire to start up a great enterprise very soon, and this time you'll be absolutely determined to succeed.

November at a Glance

LOVE	❤	❤	❤	❤	❤
WORK	★	★	★		
MONEY	£				
HEALTH	✚	✚	✚	✚	✚
LUCK	♘	♘	♘	♘	♘

SUNDAY, 1ST NOVEMBER
Mercury into Sagittarius

Mercury moves into the area of your chart that deals with duties and health. This suggests that if you have been feeling unwell, the healing effects of this planet will soon ensure that you are feeling better soon. The chances are that any health problems affecting you and your loved ones will soon pass.

MONDAY, 2ND NOVEMBER
Void Moon

There are no important planetary aspects today, and even the Moon is unaspected. This kind of a day is called a 'void of course Moon' day, because the Moon is void of aspects during this part of its course. The best way to approach such a day is to do what is normal and natural for you without starting anything new or particularly special.

TUESDAY, 3RD NOVEMBER
Moon square Neptune

It would be too easy to make promises that you have no intention of keeping today, just to keep the peace! However, these vows will be remembered and someone close will expect you to honour your word.

WEDNESDAY, 4TH NOVEMBER
Full Moon

The Full Moon could make you feel tense and it could also bring you an unexpected expense which, when you come to think of it, is probably only to be expected. The best thing to do today is to jog along as usual and don't get caught up in anyone else's bad mood.

THURSDAY, 5TH NOVEMBER
Moon trine Neptune

Today should be a social extravaganza for you and for someone special in your life. Don't be a pair of wallflowers, get out into the social whirl and have a ball!

FRIDAY, 6TH NOVEMBER
Mercury conjunct Pluto

Someone's got to take the lead at work and it looks as though it's going to be you! After all, you have the gift of the gab now and can persuade anyone to do anything. So, if you are elected spokesperson, either with without your consent, you'll do an excellent job. Don't stray far from the telephone or fax machine.

SATURDAY, 7TH NOVEMBER
Mars opposite Jupiter

Stop, think and decide if you really need to make that journey today. If you can put off any kind of travel for the next few days, then do so. If you need to get in touch with anybody, be diplomatic and keep your temper in check.

SUNDAY, 8TH NOVEMBER
Venus trine Jupiter

Some of you could soon enjoy a serious liaison with a rather exotic foreigner and, while this opens your eyes to many new and interesting ideas, you may also find yourself being swept along just that bit too fast. A letter from a faraway place may offer a change of lifestyle, but you need to look at this carefully and practically.

MONDAY, 9TH NOVEMBER
Venus sextile Mars

The excellent aspect of Venus and Mars can only mean one thing … and that's romance! Words of love are about to be spoken. Of course, how seriously you take them is up to you. You can at least expect some flirting today, especially when travelling.

TUESDAY, 10TH NOVEMBER
Sun trine Jupiter

You could acquire something very important soon. This could be as big an item as a new home or a vehicle of some description. You will enjoy working hard for these concrete rewards, especially as you know that others appreciate your efforts. A charismatic and exciting person will brighten up your working life and perhaps your personal life, too.

WEDNESDAY, 11TH NOVEMBER
Moon square Venus

You may need to work out a sensible budget in order to obtain all the things you need in the future. Despite the fact that Venus is tempting you into spending money on luxuries now, don't give in – stick to your decision and keep your eye on your goals. Women may try to throw their weight around today and, while their behaviour is irritating, these ladies do seem to have a point that is worth noting.

THURSDAY, 12TH NOVEMBER
Moon square Pluto

It will be very hard to get anywhere today, possibly in a literal sense in that your vehicle's off the road or that the person who promised you a lift has let you down. If there isn't a genuine travel problem, then you will simply face frustrations in your daily chores. Obstacles will arise due to circumstances beyond your control.

FRIDAY, 13TH NOVEMBER
Jupiter direct

Many of your convictions have gone through profound changes since Jupiter went retrograde. Today, the giant planet resumes its direct course and you can take stock of the situation. A lot of confusion will now be resolved and you may feel that your luck improves as your mind clears.

SATURDAY, 14TH NOVEMBER
Sun sextile Mars

If you're the sporty type, this is the day for you! The Sun is in splendid aspect to Mars, so any form of competition, from racing to scrabble, is favoured. Remember that it's not the winning but the taking part that counts, even if you are something of a bad loser!

SUNDAY, 15TH NOVEMBER
Moon sextile Mercury

This is a 'down-to-earth-with-a-bump' day, on which thoughts of love, travel to distant realms and any other kind of exotic dreams are displaced by the need to get on with the chores. Housework may be the order of the day (for both sexes) or you may have to do some making and mending around the home. If you have a job, the same seems to apply there; duty all the way.

MONDAY, 16TH NOVEMBER
Moon opposite Saturn

You seem to be in a phase where it is hard for you to reconcile matters related to home and work. Home life is probably trolling along fairly peacefully, but work may be awkward so you may find it hard to balance both sets of demands. For instance, your employers may want you to work unsociable hours or to start work at a time that is awkward for your family.

TUESDAY, 17TH NOVEMBER
Venus into Sagittarius

Any squabbles at work should be resolved by the entry of Venus into your Solar house of habits, effort and service to others. Colleagues will get on better with each other from now on, for a spirit of harmony becomes as important in the workplace as in the home. If you're self-employed or earn your living by means of your wits, the presence of Venus is very encouraging for your future prospects. You'll find that the influence of women is more important from now on.

WEDNESDAY, 18TH NOVEMBER
Moon trine Jupiter

It's time to think ahead. Your personal life needs some attention and you need to feel satisfied with what you do, so creativity and innovation are important now. A holiday would be just the ticket. If you're attached, then this break away could renew your relationship. If not, a holiday romance should fit the bill.

THURSDAY, 19TH NOVEMBER
New Moon

This month's New Moon is in an area of your chart that deals with artistic pursuits, so if there's something you want to do in this field now is the time to get started. For some of you this could be as important as making a home, starting a family or beginning a business enterprise. Younger members of the family could also show signs of creativity now.

FRIDAY, 20TH NOVEMBER
Mercury square Jupiter

Just because you want a quiet time today it won't be wise to fob off others with easy promises that you have no intention of honouring. This isn't the way to keep your friends or your credibility. Of course you may think that you'll keep your word, but events out of your control decree otherwise. Keep your thoughts to yourself.

SATURDAY, 21ST NOVEMBER
Mercury retrograde

You must keep an eye on health matters now, possibly because you or one of your loved ones is feeling out of sorts. You may be working with sick people or animals at the moment and one way or another, matters related to health will be a priority. You'll also need to concentrate on duties and fulfilling other people's obligations

SUNDAY, 22ND NOVEMBER
Sun into Sagittarius

The movement of the Sun into your Solar sixth house of work signals a period of success in your endeavours. Whatever you do will have a patina of success and glamour about it now, and you will be the envy of other less fortunate or hard-working souls. Don't allow their envy to diminish your confidence.

CANCER

MONDAY, 23RD NOVEMBER
Venus conjunct Pluto

You could be quite obsessive about a health matter today. A small problem could be blown out of all proportion if you listen to half-baked ideas without knowing all the facts. If you are worried, then go to see your doctor if only to set your mind at rest.

TUESDAY, 24TH NOVEMBER
Moon sextile Sun

You are in tune with your innermost self today. Whether you are involved in your daily round of duties or struggling with complicated forms and financial arrangements, you'll be clear-sighted and totally capable. Even with the most intimate matters your tact, diplomacy and sense of justice will untangle the most complex knot.

WEDNESDAY, 25TH NOVEMBER
Venus sextile Uranus

Love could blossom in the most unlikely places as Venus makes contact with unpredictable Uranus today. A sudden whirlwind romance is forecast for many. Apart from the passionate side of things, financial good fortune is also possible.

THURSDAY, 26TH NOVEMBER
Moon sextile Saturn

There could be good things going on in connection with work or business today. Other people may come up with money-making schemes that are worth investigating. This may lead to some kind of working partnership that will stand the test of time. This may not affect you directly, but could, for example, apply to your partner.

FRIDAY, 27TH NOVEMBER
Neptune into Aquarius

Neptune's entry into one of the deepest and most secret areas of your horoscope emphasizes parts of your complex mind that you scarcely knew existed. Many of you may have psychic or spiritual experiences in the coming months.

SATURDAY, 28TH NOVEMBER
Mars trine Neptune

Murphy's Law may be in operation today, but it doesn't seem to matter. You may be in the wrong place at the wrong time, only to find that it turns out to be the right place for all the wrong reasons. If you can make sense out of all this confusion, you will be able to deal with that vague and muddled planet, Neptune.

SUNDAY, 29TH NOVEMBER
Sun conjunct Pluto

The Solar conjunction with Pluto highlights many of your habits and your health. All of us have habits that are injurious to our well-being but these are becoming noticeable in your case – at least to you! Stress is possibly a factor here. Since Pluto is the planet of transformation, this could be a golden opportunity to get rid of some of the problems in your life. A more positive, healthy attitude could emerge from this astral event.

MONDAY, 30TH NOVEMBER
Moon conjunct Saturn

You will have to get down to some hard work and some serious attention to detail today because Saturn, the taskmaster of the zodiac, is chasing your tail. Your boss may want a long and complicated job done by the end of the day and you may have to stay late in order to finish it. If you have a lot to do in the home, it could be a late night.

December at a Glance

LOVE	❤	❤	❤	❤	❤
WORK	★				
MONEY	£	£			
HEALTH	✛	✛	✛	✛	✛
LUCK	♘	♘	♘		

TUESDAY, 1ST DECEMBER
Mercury sextile Uranus

You are likely to have a lot on your plate today, but this shouldn't cause you any concern. You'll have the mental and physical energy to accomplish a great deal now so there should be very little to make you pause in your rush for success.

CANCER

WEDNESDAY, 2ND DECEMBER
Sun sextile Uranus

Anyone who thought that they knew you inside out will be amazed today as you throw off the shackles of convention and do something that you've longed to do for ages! You won't care what others think, since you'll know that what you're doing is right!

THURSDAY, 3RD DECEMBER
Full Moon

Apart from a Full Moon today there is not much going on in the planetary scene. Therefore, rest and relax, take it easy and do only what you really have to do. You may feel the need to examine your heart and mind and embark on an inward journey to analyse your actions and options. This may result in a few changes being made.

FRIDAY, 4TH DECEMBER
Moon opposite Venus

You could be feeling a bit off-colour today and women readers will probably be affected by their hormones. Try not to take on anything difficult or demanding and just get through what needs to be done as best you can. Whatever your sex – or your problem – go to bed early with a hot water bottle and a stiff drink!

SATURDAY, 5TH DECEMBER
Mercury sextile Mars

It's a housework day, but before you despair we'll just add that you won't be alone in this long and thankless task. In fact, you are likely to whip your family into shape and share out the jobs in order of difficulty. You may be a domestic tyrant, but you will get things done!

SUNDAY, 6TH DECEMBER
Moon trine Jupiter

With the added encouragement of Jupiter in your house of adventure and travel, the Moon urges movement in your life, so this is not a day to sit at home knitting. Get out and about, meet people, go sightseeing. In short, anything that gives a new experience is favoured now. If you don't feel that you can just take off, then read a good book or watch an interesting documentary. Your mind needs some stimulation, so give in to it.

CANCER

MONDAY, 7TH DECEMBER
Moon sextile Mars

The Moon makes a good aspect to Mars today, so for those who are working the career picture looks promising. This is not a time to ignore material affairs such as pension plans, insurance policies and all sorts of shared resources. A little attention paid to your long-term security will reap ample dividends.

TUESDAY, 8TH DECEMBER
Moon trine Sun

You have a clear idea of what is important to you today, and you know just what your priorities are. Fortunately those around you also seem to have the same values and priorities, so it will be easy to get through your work.

WEDNESDAY, 9TH DECEMBER
Venus trine Saturn

You'll really feel that you are getting somewhere today and the efforts you have made in the past are about to pay off. That's not to say that you can slacken, but there's a light at the end of the tunnel.

THURSDAY, 10TH DECEMBER
Moon square Sun

It won't be a good idea to overload your schedule too much today. We know you're bounding with self-confidence, but your energy levels just aren't high enough at present. If you're working, the evening won't come around fast enough. If not, then leave domestic chores for now. A few unwashed dishes won't matter.

FRIDAY, 11TH DECEMBER
Venus into Capricorn

Close emotional links will flourish now as Venus, planet of love, enters your horoscopic area of partnerships. If you're in any doubt about your relationship, then this is the time to show your affection in no uncertain terms. In more practical concerns Venus adds goodwill in business dealings, while the next few weeks could see the transformation of a rival in commerce or love to an ally and friend. Those who are single may find the man or woman of their dreams.

SATURDAY, 12TH DECEMBER
Mars sextile Pluto

Even difficult tasks can be accomplished today when everyone in your family puts their shoulders to the wheel. You may have to play boss a little to get there, but even so the atmosphere should be good-natured.

SUNDAY, 13TH DECEMBER
Moon sextile Sun

Duty may call today, but you'll rush back home at the earliest opportunity. You'll be happiest in your own environment, basking in a harmonious family atmosphere.

MONDAY, 14TH DECEMBER
Moon sextile Venus

It is amazing the difference a helpful person makes. The Lunar aspect to Venus today provides advice, sound information and a pleasant smile. Women especially will go out of their way to assist you.

TUESDAY, 15TH DECEMBER
Mars trine Uranus

Your financial fortunes may look uncertain, but an unexpected event could easily make good the losses you have experienced. Keep your head and be prepared to act quickly to benefit from any financial opportunity.

WEDNESDAY, 16TH DECEMBER
Moon sextile Neptune

A sudden declaration of love is not unlikely today. Emotions are very close to the surface, and no matter how you repress them, they are still likely to bubble over into many areas of your life. Apart from the physical aspect, you'll experience deep spiritual desire.

THURSDAY, 17TH DECEMBER
Moon sextile Uranus

You may hit upon an idea for something that makes you look and feel better, such as the soothing effects of essential oils. You may find something good to eat or some kind of beauty product that clears your complexion or makes you feel better. Even if there is nothing new for you to try, treat yourself to a luxurious soak in your favourite bubble bath, and relax.

FRIDAY, 18TH DECEMBER
New Moon

This is definitely a time for very positive new beginnings in connection with work. Therefore you could look for a new job now or be given a promotion or a rise in salary. You seem to be more interested in work-related matters than for some time past, and your imagination may be captured by some kind of money-making scheme. You may also find a way of making your work life easier.

CANCER

SATURDAY, 19TH DECEMBER
Sun trine Saturn

There'll be no stopping you today! Your sense of purpose will be strong in all career-related matters, and you'll be determined to succeed. You can be sure that your efforts will not go unnoticed by those who matter.

SUNDAY, 20TH DECEMBER
Moon square Mars

Your partner may be feeling irritable today, and the chances are that he or she has had more than enough of the home, the family, cooking, eating and clearing up. Take pity on yourself and your partner and go out for a meal, or walk the dog and the kids and enjoy a breath of fresh air.

MONDAY, 21ST DECEMBER
Mercury conjunct Pluto

Subtle persuasion is your forte today and you can convince bosses and work colleagues that black is white, if you are so inclined. Behind this silver-tongued charm there is a stark purpose. You'll be determined to get your own way, and since direct methods aren't likely to work, some soft soap and manipulation should do the trick.

TUESDAY, 22ND DECEMBER
Sun into Capricorn

The Sun moves into your Solar house of partnerships from today so you'll be caught up in a romantic atmosphere that'll be difficult, if not impossible, to resist. If you are married or involved in a close relationship, then this influence will tend to deepen your commitment and add to your happiness. If, however, you're single, the next few weeks could easily see someone special entering your life.

WEDNESDAY, 23RD DECEMBER
Mercury sextile Uranus

Good news concerning work and money prospects is on the cards today. Mercury and Uranus combine to bring a very welcome bolt from the blue which will certainly put a smile on your face.

THURSDAY, 24TH DECEMBER
Moon square Pluto

You may be feeling off-colour this Christmas Eve or you may be overwhelmed with last-minute shopping. Either way, this is not the best of days on which to get anything done so it's worth knocking off early and spending the evening resting.

You may find that others are being manipulative or even completely untruthful to you today, so don't take too much notice of them. Have an early night tonight … think of tomorrow!

FRIDAY, 25TH DECEMBER
Moon conjunct Jupiter

Your self-belief may be tested at some point this Christmas Day, and it's important that you stand firm. The Moon conjuncts Jupiter now and this sets your sights on affairs in distant parts of the world. You can't be bothered with petty worries and small-minded attitudes; you have bigger, better concepts to dwell on as well as the spirit of the season.

SATURDAY, 26TH DECEMBER
Moon square Sun

This is one of those days when you wish you had stayed in bed! There are potential difficulties all around you now and it will take all your attempts at tact and charm to get others to behave decently. All those who should, by rights, be on your side will lack any urge to co-operate, and your usual sources of human kindness will have simply dried up.

SUNDAY, 27TH DECEMBER
Moon square Venus

For such a forward-thinking person it may come as something of a shock to discover that you're starting to lag behind the times. You may feel that you've fallen into a rut. Of course, you've achieved so much that you're entitled to a little comfort, but you're also a person who craves a challenge. This is a time to think about changes in your career.

MONDAY, 28TH DECEMBER
Mercury sextile Mars

Forthright speech and actions are the key to success now. In both work and family affairs, beating around the bush will get you nowhere. If someone needs to be pulled into line then state your case clearly, and without losing your temper.

TUESDAY, 29TH DECEMBER
Saturn direct

Saturn turns to direct motion today in your Solar tenth house of aims and ambitions. This will make it easier for you to achieve whatever you are striving for. It is true that you are having to work hard to reach your goals, but now that Saturn is no longer travelling backwards you'll begin to see some real progress.

WEDNESDAY, 30TH DECEMBER

Moon trine Neptune

Your mind is turning inwards at the moment and you might be concentrating on things that are outside your normal routine. You may find yourself thinking about religion, the occult or even the more serious aspects of astrology. Artistic or creative subjects may inspire you and you could begin your own project, visit a gallery or enjoy listening to some good music.

THURSDAY, 31ST DECEMBER

Moon trine Mars

Youngish men will prove to be helpful and useful today. You may have to call out someone to mend an item in your home, and just the right guy will come along to help you out. You could consider buying some labour-saving devices, although you may prefer to keep your plans to yourself for now. Aside from this, have a very happy New Year's Eve!

1999

January at a Glance

LOVE	❤			
WORK	★			
MONEY	£	£	£	
HEALTH	✪	✪	✪	✪
LUCK	∪	∪		

FRIDAY, 1ST JANUARY

Mercury square Jupiter

Just because you want a quiet time on New Year's day it isn't wise to fob others off with easy promises that you've no intention of keeping. This isn't the way to keep friends or even any credibility. Of course you may think that your words will be fulfilled, but events out of your control decree otherwise, so keep your lip zipped.

SATURDAY, 2ND JANUARY
Full Moon

The Full Moon in your sign shows that you've come to the end of a personal phase and that it's time to tie up the loose ends and move on. This should be an opportunity to rid yourself of harmful little habits and create a whole new persona. This could be an image transformation. So, if you're at all dissatisfied by the way you present yourself to the world then work out your own personal make-over. You'll be astounded by the reception the new you gets.

SUNDAY, 3RD JANUARY
Moon opposite Venus

Someone very close to you is feeling a terrible burden of insecurity now. It may be that some harsh facts recently faced have shaken confidence. Some reassurance from you is now vital. Remember that you too can be prone to over-sensitivity so have some sympathy with one who needs your presence now.

MONDAY, 4TH JANUARY
Venus into Aquarius

Venus enters the area of your chart that is closely involved with love and sex today. Oddly enough, this aspect can bring the end of a difficult relationship or, just as easily begin a wonderful new one. If you have been dating but haven't yet got around to "mating", this could be the start of something wonderful. Your emotional life over the next two or three weeks should be something to remember, that's for sure!

TUESDAY, 5TH JANUARY
Venus conjunct Neptune

You seem to be getting on to a better wavelength with those who are around you. It seems that they have been harbouring dreams, ideas and plans for the future that may be in conflict with your own. However, if you were to sit down and talk things over now you may be able to reach a compromise that gives everyone something to be happy with. Your partner is in a particularly romantic frame of mind now and that will help your cause for the moment at least.

WEDNESDAY, 6TH JANUARY
Moon square Pluto

It will be hard to get anywhere today, possibly in the sense that your vehicle is off the road or that the person who promised you a lift has let you down. If there isn't a genuine travel problem, then you will face frustrations in your daily life and obstacles being put in your way by circumstances that are beyond your control.

THURSDAY, 7TH JANUARY
Mercury into Capricorn

The inquisitive Mercury moves into your Solar house of marriage and long-lasting relationships from today ushering in a period when a renewed understanding can be reached between yourself and your partner. New relationships can be formed under this influence too, though these will tend to be on a light, fairly superficial level. Good humour and plenty of charm should be a feature for a few weeks, though you must try to curb a tendency to needlessly criticize another's foibles. Remember, not even you are perfect!

FRIDAY, 8TH JANUARY
Moon trine Venus

A truly romantic interlude could turn into real passion today. You seem to have the kind of magnetic charisma that's guaranteed to make you irresistible to the opposite sex. Even if all you end up doing is sitting about at home with your loved one, make this as sexy and loving an occasion as you can. Set the scene with perfume, dim lights and sexy music on the magic music machine tonight!

SATURDAY, 9TH JANUARY
Moon square Sun

You aren't in the most active of moods today. The Moon's square aspect to the Sun ensures that you'll be happiest within your home environment. You won't want to tax your system at all, so a day of lounging about is your idea of bliss. Of course, there are domestic duties too, but you're likely to rely on the goodwill of your other half to carry out those. Don't be surprised if your lazy attitude is resented.

SUNDAY, 10TH JANUARY
Moon opposite Saturn

Your parents could cause you some worry today and if you haven't got parents of your own, there could be worry and difficulties in connection with older people in your circle. They may be ill and needing help, or they may be tiresome and demanding for no particular reason at all. You will have to work out whether you spend the day running around after these people or whether you leave them to get on with things by themselves.

MONDAY, 11TH JANUARY
Moon square Uranus

You could be held back by an unexpected hiccup in the home today. Just when you had got everything running very smoothly, some kind of problem will occur.

You may drop or break something valuable or useful, or your children could destroy something that you value. Something that normally never gives trouble could suddenly go on the blink just at the wrong moment.

TUESDAY, 12TH JANUARY
Venus sextile Pluto

Partnership affairs are likely to be extremely fulfilling and quite profitable today. The combined energies of Venus and Pluto change established rules and put you on a new footing with an employer or colleague. The alteration in work practices will be a harmonious and natural progression and will work to your mutual benefit.

WEDNESDAY, 13TH JANUARY
Venus conjunct Uranus

This is the time when you could find yourself making a major commitment to somebody else either in connection with a business matter or a loving and romantic one. There is likely to be something off-beat or unusual about any such relationship, but that only seems to add to the fun of it. You may have a stroke of luck where business or money is concerned.

THURSDAY, 14TH JANUARY
Sun sextile Jupiter

It just goes to show that you aren't all bad. It's fortunate that after some irritable outburst there is someone who understands and still believes in you. It's obvious that you are an important pillar in someone else's life so respond with affection now.

FRIDAY, 15TH JANUARY
Sun square Mars

Tempers are rather frayed today, and those around you are not the only ones at fault! You too are simmering and your rage is likely to boil over quite soon. Domestic and relationship issues are likely to be extremely irritating now, but do try to exercise some self-control.

SATURDAY, 16TH JANUARY
Moon conjunct Mercury

Spend today in the company of someone you love. You need some emotional reassurance and can only get it by an affectionate heart-to-heart. The beginnings of any sort of partnership, romantic or business is strongly favoured today.

S U N D A Y , 1 7 T H J A N U A R Y
New Moon

The only planetary activity today is a new Moon in your opposite sign. It is possible that this could bring the start of a new relationship for the lonely but, to be honest, this planetary aspect is a bit too weak for such a big event. It is much more likely that you will improve on a current relationship rather than start a new one at this time.

M O N D A Y , 1 8 T H J A N U A R Y
Sun square Saturn

If it is possible, get away for a holiday or take time off in order to concentrate on your social life. The reason for this is that you seem to be in the kind of phase where it is impossible to climb the ladder of success. The best thing to do, therefore, is to leave it, take a holiday or simply coast along until a more auspicious time.

T U E S D A Y , 1 9 T H J A N U A R Y
Moon conjunct Venus

This should be an intensely passionate time as the influence on Venus is triggered by the conjunction with the Moon. Your sex life is due to be boosted in a most delightful way. Apart from the physical advantages of the conjunction it also works to your economic advantage. Contracts, and financial agreements are bound to work in your favour.

W E D N E S D A Y , 2 0 T H J A N U A R Y
Sun into Aquarius

Today, the Sun enters your Solar eighth house of beginnings and endings. Thus, over the next month, you can expect something to wind its way to a conclusion, while something else starts to take its place. This doesn't seem to signify a major turning point or any really big event in your life but it does mark one of those small turning points that we all go through from time to time.

T H U R S D A Y , 2 1 S T J A N U A R Y
Mars opposite Saturn

This is not the day in which to take on those who are in positions of power or authority over you. It would be better to let sleeping bosses lie or to leave things as they are. If you try to change the *status quo* in any way, you will come a cropper. It may be that you are right in your thinking but others will simply not be ready to see things the way that you do now.

FRIDAY, 22ND JANUARY
Sun conjunct Neptune

You are in an escapist mood today and you may not be the only one. It seems that your partner is also feeling like getting away from it all. You may be strongly drawn to water now, so take a visit to any local beauty spot that is close to water or anywhere that overlooks a body of water. You and your lover will find this spiritually refreshing.

SATURDAY, 23RD JANUARY
Mercury sextile Jupiter

It just goes to show that you aren't all bad and it is fortunate that after some irritable outburst, there is someone who understands and still believes in you. It is obvious that you are an important pillar in someone else's life so respond with some affection now.

SUNDAY, 24TH JANUARY
Mercury square Saturn

You may be torn between the demands of your job and the needs of your partner today. On the other hand, you may be filled with great ideas, only to find that you are prevented from putting them into action. To be honest, today shouldn't be all that hard but you may have to make quite an effort in order to make all the component parts of your life function properly.

MONDAY, 25TH JANUARY
Moon square Uranus

If you have made complicated plans to do something with your friends today, you will have to disappoint them and maybe even abandon the whole idea. You may be off-colour or simply not in the mood to socialize today. You could hear some slightly upsetting news about a friend and this will also tend to make you feel a bit down. You may be in a tense and touchy mood today.

TUESDAY, 26TH JANUARY
Mars into Scorpio

Mars moves into a very creative area of your chart now, so if there is a project that you would like to get started upon, Mars will give you the drive and energy with which to do it. This is a good day for any kind of sporting or energetic pursuit so, if you want to practise your skills or get ready for some kind of future competition, then get down to it today.

CANCER

WEDNESDAY, 27TH JANUARY
Venus sextile Saturn

You could be feeling frisky today, with more than your usual amount of passion in mind. Unfortunately, this could add up to frustration since chilly Saturn is set to pour cold water on your amorous intent.

THURSDAY, 28TH JANUARY
Venus into Pisces

Venus enters your Solar ninth house of exploration this month and this may make you slightly restless. Venus is concerned with the pleasures of life and also with leisure activities of all kinds, so explore such ideas as your sporting interests or, perhaps of listening to interesting music or going to art galleries and the like. You may want to travel somewhere new and interesting soon.

FRIDAY, 29TH JANUARY
Venus trine Mars

A romantic atmosphere prevails today as Mars and Venus inspire love divine. If you are single, you will be prone to sudden attraction and wild infatuation today, while those who are already linked should take advantage of the passionate vibes to rekindle some of the old magic in your relationship. A trip to a memorable location could play a part in affairs of the heart now.

SATURDAY, 30TH JANUARY
Sun sextile Pluto

If you've been disturbed by behind-the-scenes activities at work, the Solar influence should dispel many of your fears today. You could learn a surprising truth and if so keep it to yourself for the moment. Discretion is the key in many areas now. In intimate affairs too, secrecy is vital.

SUNDAY, 31ST JANUARY
Full Moon eclipse

Something will come to a head today and this may even cause an argument amongst family members. There may have been disagreements over money recently and now it seems that these simmering disagreements are destined to come to a full rolling boil. You must stand your ground and prevent others from manipulating you into actions that will work against your best long-term interests.

February at a Glance

LOVE	♥	♥		
WORK	★			
MONEY	£	£	£	
HEALTH	✛	✛	✛	
LUCK	∪	∪	∪	

MONDAY, 1ST FEBRUARY
Mars square Neptune

Being too hasty with money would be a big mistake today! You might think that you can comfortably afford to indulge a hobby but the true, and possibly hidden costs will be enormous. Think again!

TUESDAY, 2ND FEBRUARY
Sun conjunct Uranus

Though you are generally in favour of the *status quo*, today you'll be gripped by a revolutionary zeal. You'll want to see changes, not in the distant future but now! Unfortunately, the world seems unlikely to move at your desired pace so you could end the day rather frustrated.

WEDNESDAY, 3RD FEBRUARY
Sun conjunct Mercury

Approach contracts and agreements with caution today. That's not to say that they are bad things to get involved with, just that you've got to play your cards close to your chest to make the most of them. You have the ability to handle any negotiations with ease since your shrewd appreciation of realities gives you the edge over any opponents. You'll have no trouble with small print.

THURSDAY, 4TH FEBRUARY
Moon opposite Jupiter

It's a very restless day as the Moon opposes Jupiter. You're likely to feel bored and stifled by the familiar now and yearn for a little adventure. Travel may be fraught with delays though, so it may be wisest to confine yourself to expanding your knowledge via reading rather than risking a traffic jam.

CANCER

FRIDAY, 5TH FEBRUARY
Mercury conjunct Uranus

Someone who you are in partnership with will have one or two astoundingly bright ideas today. This may be in connection with a business matter or it may be that you are trying to find answers to purely private and personal problems. Love could strike the unwary, especially if you find yourself in the company of new and interesting faces or if you find yourself in new and interesting places.

SATURDAY, 6TH FEBRUARY
Venus square Pluto

Your personal desires for freedom and irresponsibility have to be placed on the back burner today. Venus's harsh aspect to Pluto shows that the daily drudgery is getting you down, yet it would be very unwise to fly the nest. The repercussions of such an action would be far-reaching and very damaging.

SUNDAY, 7TH FEBRUARY
Moon conjunct Mars

Your entire chart is energized by the Moon's conjunction with Mars today. This should inspire and activate all the romantic potentials in your life. The trouble is that you could get a little big-headed now, so you'll have to guard against being just a shade too forceful especially with a lover. Don't be too impulsive and domineering and you won't spoil the splendid day.

MONDAY, 8TH FEBRUARY
Moon square Sun

Personal desires and the expectations of others will tend to clash under the stressful aspect of the Moon and Sun. Accounts, contracts and paperwork have to be dealt with before you can take any time off.

TUESDAY, 9TH FEBRUARY
Moon trine Jupiter

A convivial atmosphere takes hold as the Moon contacts Jupiter, spreading a little happiness around you. Negative moods are now forgiven and forgotten as harmonious influences lift your spirits. You could make a special effort to show the more romantic side to your nature and take some time out for an intimate celebration to remember.

WEDNESDAY, 10TH FEBRUARY
Moon sextile Uranus

Pleasant surprises are on the way today and these will be of benefit to your working life and also that of your partner or lover. You may be given an unexpected bonus or a commendation of some kind as a result of work that you have done in the past. You may meet up unexpectedly with a friend whom you haven't seen for some time and this could even lead to some kind of joint activity for you both in the future.

THURSDAY, 11TH FEBRUARY
Mercury sextile Saturn

A word to the wise is generally considered enough, and that's the way it is today. A quiet chat to an employer should provide you with a hint of what is to come. Keep the information to yourself and profit by it when the opportunity arises.

FRIDAY, 12TH FEBRUARY
Mercury into Pisces

Mercury enters your Solar house of adventure and philosophy from today and stimulates your curiosity. Everything from international affairs to religious questions will tax your mind. Your desire to travel will be boosted for a few weeks, as indeed will a need to expand your knowledge, perhaps by taking up a course at a local college. Keep an open mind. Allow yourself encounters with new ideas.

SATURDAY, 13TH FEBRUARY
Jupiter into Aries

You are about to start a new phase which will be with you for the next year or so. This will enhance your job prospects and allow you to make the kind of money that you need. Your status out in the world will increase and you will become quite well known in your particular field of work. You may travel in search of work or start to spread your net wider in some way.

SUNDAY, 14TH FEBRUARY
Moon sextile Jupiter

Your fast thinking could save the day for someone in a position of authority today and this, in turn, could open a doorway of opportunity for you, so be prepared to take advantage of bosses' goodwill. You could take a stride up the ladder of professional success now simply because you know how to keep a secret.

MONDAY, 15TH FEBRUARY
Moon conjunct Uranus

You should have some kind of totally unexpected stroke of luck today. The only problem is that it hard to see just which direction this is coming from. The chances are that your partner or a close associate will be responsible for helping you or for bringing the lucky event about. There may be great news about a contract or a legal document of some kind, especially if concerns money in some way.

TUESDAY, 16TH FEBRUARY
New Moon eclipse

There is a new Moon eclipse in the area of your chart which is devoted to joint matters today. This could make you face up to the fact that one joint arrangement is no longer viable. It may be a business partnership or a personal relationship that is causing trouble and you may reach the unhappy conclusion that this cannot go on any longer. It is possible to change a bad situation but you will have to do so firmly rather than to simply hope that it will get better all by itself.

WEDNESDAY, 17TH FEBRUARY
Sun sextile Saturn

You could find yourself in the position of supporting and generally advising a person of authority today. This boss or official is feeling somewhat insecure so it's up to you to shoulder his or her burden for a short while. Take this task on gladly because you won't lose out in the long run.

THURSDAY, 18TH FEBRUARY
Mercury square Pluto

If you feel hemmed in or restricted by duty and drudgery, a lot of the resentment you feel will come bubbling to the surface today. Why indeed should you shoulder all the burdens when there are perfectly able-bodied souls around who should be doing their share? Stand up for yourself!

FRIDAY, 19TH FEBRUARY
Sun into Pisces

The Sun moves into your Solar ninth house today and it will stay there for a month. This would be a good time to travel overseas or to explore new neighbourhoods. It is also a good time to take up an interest in spiritual matters. You may find yourself keen to read about religious or philosophical subjects or even to explore the world of psychic healing over the next month or so.

SATURDAY, 20TH FEBRUARY
Void Moon

This is one of those days when none of the planets is making any worthwhile kind of aspect to any of the others. Even the Moon is 'void of course', which means that it is not making any aspects of any importance to any of the other planets.

On such a day, avoid starting anything new and don't set out to do anything important. Do what needs to be done and take some time off for a rest.

SUNDAY, 21ST FEBRUARY
Venus into Aries

Venus moves into your Solar house of ambition and prominence from today. If you're involved in any career in the arts, beautification, entertainment or public relations then you're bound to do well over the next few weeks. Those who work for women bosses won't do badly either since a female influence in the workplace will aid your ambitions. Since Venus is the planet of charisma use diplomacy to solve professional problems. You can hardly fail to win with such a capacity for charm.

MONDAY, 22ND FEBRUARY
Venus sextile Neptune

Venus and Neptune are both sexy and romantic planets and at the moment they are in a good aspect to one another. Your love life may take off like a rocket today, or you may simply feel in a more sexy and amorous mood than usual. It would be a good idea to stay at home and keep your partner company with a cuddle on the sofa or a shared bath to add to the fun.

TUESDAY, 23RD FEBRUARY
Moon opposite Pluto

An opposition between the Moon and Pluto in the health areas of your chart suggest that you may be feeling under the weather today. If so, take care of yourself and don't overdo things. Pluto is not associated with accidents or acute ailments; it is far more likely to bring a chronic or on-going situation to the fore and it is particularly associated with problems in the reproductive organs.

WEDNESDAY, 24TH FEBRUARY
Venus conjunct Jupiter

This is a time of supreme good fortune on the professional front as those two benign planets, Venus and Jupiter, meet up in your Solar house of ambition and progress. If you've got any interviews planned, then you can't fail to make a good impression with those who matter. Try for a new, more satisfying job, go for promotion, because the aura of luck about you points the way to great success.

THURSDAY, 25TH FEBRUARY
Moon trine Sun

Though you may feel that your dose of luck today is too good to be true, as the day goes on you'll learn to trust the good fortune that comes your way. Your true aims and ideals look far more likely to be fulfilled than they have in a long time. Your partner is in tune with your desires, and friends show their support and goodwill. What could be better to start you off on an optimistic phase of achievement.

FRIDAY, 26TH FEBRUARY
Sun trine Mars
A good day for travelling and also for sporting activities. The combination of the Sun and Mars gives you the urge to be on the move so anything that keeps you too long in any one pace will be resented.

SATURDAY, 27TH FEBRUARY
Jupiter sextile Neptune
Today's stars bring to light an opportunity that has been previously unseen. This could come as a stunning revelation and provide a significant turning point in your life.

SUNDAY, 28TH FEBRUARY
Moon opposite Uranus
You could be facing a real conflict over money or possessions just now. You and a current or an ex-partner may be locking horns over who owns what or who is supposed to pay for what. You may need to take this to a detached outsider in order to achieve a fair settlement between you. It may not be this serious, but you do need to sort out who pays for what and how today.

March at a Glance

LOVE	❤	❤	❤		
WORK	★	★	★		
MONEY	£	£			
HEALTH	✛	✛	✛	✛	✛
LUCK	U	U	U		

CANCER

MONDAY, 1ST MARCH
Saturn into Taurus

Saturn enters your eleventh Solar house of hopes and desires today for a stay of over two years. During this time you'll find that some old friends will leave your circle as other, more mature people enter it. Your true aims will be clarified and your social conscience will become more important as an issue in your life.

TUESDAY, 2ND MARCH
Mercury into Aries

There's a certain flexibility entering your career structure as indicated by the presence of Mercury in your Solar area of ambition from today. You can now turn your acute mind to all sorts of career problems and solve them to everyone's satisfaction, and your own personal advantage. Your powers of persuasion will be heightened from now on, ensuring that you charm bosses and employers to get your own way. Those seeking work should attend interviews because your personality will shine.

WEDNESDAY, 3RD MARCH
Venus trine Pluto

This is a great day for work and whether you are trying to get some major career move off the ground, or whether you simply need to catch up with the chores in and around the home, you will achieve your objectives quite easily. A woman may help you to overcome a sticky problem and you will enjoy the atmosphere that is around you at work or, for that matter, at any place where you happen to be today.

THURSDAY, 4TH MARCH
Venus sextile Uranus

Good fortune in career affairs and in the financial stakes are indicated by today's aspect between Venus and Uranus. Apart from the more practical side of this aspect, your sex life should receive a surprising boost too. Perhaps passions will boil over in the boardroom!

FRIDAY, 5TH MARCH
Mercury sextile Neptune

If you have stood up for your rights recently, you will now be proved to have been right all along. The last person that you expect could suddenly take your side today and they could set out to prove that you had a point all along. You will be full of bright ideas today, especially the kind that can be turned into creative projects.

CANCER

SATURDAY, 6TH MARCH
Moon square Neptune

The cost of fun exceeds inflation today. What you want to do is likely to be expensive, just at a time when bills or other pressing financial demands land on your doorstep. I doubt if you'll worry about cost now – But there's always tomorrow!

SUNDAY, 7TH MARCH
Moon square Uranus

You may find it hard to please everyone today and there will definitely be too many conflicting demands being made upon you now. You may need to go somewhere on someone else's behalf and, if so, this will happen at the least convenient time. Your children may need you to be in one place, while your partner or your boss may want you to be somewhere else. You may have to accept that you can't please them all.

MONDAY, 8TH MARCH
Moon trine Venus

Your job, career or business is taking precedence just at the moment. This is probably not the time to be terribly creative or experimental in what you are doing but simply to plod along your usual path and do what you have to do. You may have nothing more exciting than household chores to occupy yourself with now but these have to be done and you might as well do them properly.

TUESDAY, 9TH MARCH
Moon trine Jupiter

After some of pressures you've been under, careerwise and in terms of burning the candle at both ends, it's time you looked at the state your physique is getting into. The Moon's aspect to Jupiter points out the benefits of a new health regime. This is a good day to work out with some aerobics, or if that's too energetic, moderate your intake with a new diet. Look after yourself.

WEDNESDAY, 10TH MARCH
Mercury retrograde

The fact that Mercury goes retrograde today throws a lot of your financial planning into confusion, and may even bring a note of embarrassment into a close relationship. There's obviously a topic which you feel impossible to approach now. At least this slow period will give you the chance to reassess both your sexual desires and the prospects of your financial fortunes. If things are going at a snail's pace now, you shouldn't be discouraged. It's for a good reason. One word of warning, don't enter any hire-purchase or other credit agreements until the middle of next month at the earliest.

THURSDAY, 11TH MARCH
Moon square Mercury

If you want any peace today, you'd better keep your mouth firmly shut because you'll get very little sympathy or understanding from others. The trouble is that you are pretty logical while those around you are too emotional to see anything rationally at all!

FRIDAY, 12TH MARCH
Moon sextile Mars

There's a bit more of that passionate intensity today. If you're attached, then the combined influences of Mars and the Moon will blow away any of the cobwebs from your relationship. Physically, you'll be very demanding, though I doubt that there'll be many objections to that trait. Love affairs, old and new are the centre of your interest now, but remember that you are rather too assertive at the moment, so try not to frighten the object of desire off before you turn out the light.

SATURDAY, 13TH MARCH
Mercury sextile Neptune

When it comes to money-making ideas you're definitely the person who is on the ball today! Your mental dexterity combines with an almost psychic grasp of the potentials for profit.

SUNDAY, 14TH MARCH
Moon sextile Pluto

This is a good time to talk over anything to do with money and your job. This may mean discussing your salary, bonus, pension schemes, tax payments or rebates or anything else to do with your earnings. This may equally well mean discussing the financial situation and the outlook for the future for the organization that you work for. Some of these discussions could be on a high corporate level.

MONDAY, 15TH MARCH
Moon sextile Venus

The link between the Moon and Venus adds a compelling and seductive quality to your nature now. Since you're quick on the uptake, it won't take you long to realize that you're in a position to twist anyone around your little finger. A small flirtation today will gain you far more than any number of confrontations.

CANCER

TUESDAY, 16TH MARCH
Moon square Pluto

This could be an awkward day for you because your mood is philosophical and laid back, while the rest of the world wants you to get down to the chores. Guard against being manoeuvred or manipulated into doing something that is against your beliefs or against your moral outlook today. For example, if someone comes into your place of work and offers you stolen goods, then don't have anything to do with it.

WEDNESDAY, 17TH MARCH
New Moon

The New Moon in your house of adventure urges you to push ahead with new projects. You're in a self-confident mood, and feel able to tackle anything the world throws at you. There's a lure of the exotic today as well, as far-off places exert a powerful attraction. Think again about widening your personal horizons, by travel or, indeed, by taking up an educational course. Intellectually you're on top form and your curiosity is boundless.

THURSDAY, 18TH MARCH
Venus into Taurus

Venus moves into your eleventh house of friendship and group activities today, bringing a few weeks of happiness and harmony for you and your friends. You could fall in love under this transit or you could reaffirm your feelings towards a current partner. You should be looking and feeling rather good now but, if not, this is a good time to spend some money on your appearance and also to do something about any nagging health problems.

FRIDAY, 19TH MARCH
Sun conjunct Mercury

If you have any kind of legal or official matter to deal with, this would be a good day to get on with it. It is a good time to sign contracts or agreements or to make a business deal. You seem to be taking a deep interest in spiritual matters now and this may be the start of something which will affect the course of your life from here on.

SATURDAY, 20TH MARCH
Venus conjunct Saturn

The comforting presence of an old friend is the main feature of the day. The embrace of Venus and Saturn in the most social area of your chart emphasizes the deep emotional values of long-lasting friendship.

CANCER

SUNDAY, 21ST MARCH
Sun into Aries

The Sun moves decisively into your horoscope area of ambition from today bringing in an month when your worldly progress will achieve absolute priority. You need to feel that what you are doing is worthwhile and has more meaning than simply paying the bills. You may feel the urge to change you career, to make a long-term commitment to a worthwhile cause, or simply to demand recognition for past efforts. However this ambitious phase manifests, you can be sure that your prospects are considerably boosted from now on.

MONDAY, 22ND MARCH
Moon trine Neptune

Your mind is turning inwards at the moment and you might be concentrating on things that are outside of your normal routine. You may find yourself thinking of such things as religion, the occult or even the more serious aspects of astrology for a while now. Artistic or creative subjects may inspire you now and you could start a project for yourself or you may go along to a gallery or to listen to some good music today.

TUESDAY, 23RD MARCH
Venus square Neptune

You'll be deeply over-sensitive today. Venus and Neptune, both weepy planets, are in bad aspect now making you prone to sentimentality. You'll be a walking shoulder to cry on if you aren't careful and everyone you know will want sympathy and understanding. It's a pity that no one seems ready to hear about your woes!

WEDNESDAY, 24TH MARCH
Moon square Sun

A world-weary mood takes a hold under a harsh Lunar aspect to the Sun today. You've put up with a lot of pressures recently, and even though the more general outlook is good you are showing the strain. The expectations others have of you are a major factor of the problem. You've done a lot for others recently, but honestly you could do with a day off.

THURSDAY, 25TH MARCH
Sun sextile Neptune

You seem to be able to see some kind of glimmering of light at the end of the tunnel now. You may be able to see a way of achieving your ends or of reaching your objectives. However, there seem to be a number of obstacles still in your way and it will take subtlety and care before you can find a way around these. One particular person could prove to be very helpful now, especially in connection with money and business.

FRIDAY, 26TH MARCH
Moon square Saturn

The influence of the planet Saturn makes you question some of your deepest assumptions today. Though the ringed orb forces a reassessment, it won't do to take a too negative view of your situation. Of course, you have anxieties but the true picture isn't as black as you paint it. Every cloud has a silver lining, so don't dwell on the grim side. Your main problem is that you've got an overactive imagination today.

SATURDAY, 27TH MARCH
Venus opposite Mars

You may fancy a quiet evening with the one you love only to find that you are constantly interrupted by visits from friends or the demands of children. Though you don't want to be rude, there is a time and a place for everything so tempers as well as other passions will become heated.

SUNDAY, 28TH MARCH
Void Moon

Occasionally one finds a day in which neither the planets nor the Moon make any major aspects to each other and on such a day, the Moon's course is said to be 'void'. There is nothing wrong with a day like this but there is no point in trying to start anything new or anything important because there isn't enough of a planetary boost to get it off the ground. Stick to your normal routine.

MONDAY, 29TH MARCH
Moon square Pluto

You could be harbouring some hidden resentments at the moment. Perhaps you feel that a colleague isn't pulling his weight, or that you have too much on your plate to cope. Keeping these feelings hidden won't solve the problem so tactfully suggest a little more effort on the part of your co-worker.

TUESDAY, 30TH MARCH
Jupiter trine Pluto

It's a hard working day in which you'll have little time to indulge yourself! If that sounds soul-destroying, then take comfort from the fact that everything you do now will be amply rewarded. Even tasks you dread will be easier than you think.

CANCER

WEDNESDAY, 31ST MARCH
Full Moon

The Full Moon today focuses firmly on family and domestic issues. Perhaps it's time for some straight talking because this is the best opportunity you'll get to put an end to home-based or emotional problems. In some ways it's time to put your cards on the table, yet equally to give credit and take some share of blame in family affairs. Apart from such personal concerns it's time to speak to someone in authority about your ambitions.

April at a Glance

LOVE	♥				
WORK	★				
MONEY	£	£	£		
HEALTH	✪	✪	✪	✪	✪
LUCK	♘	♘	♘		

THURSDAY, 1ST APRIL
Sun conjunct Jupiter

All your future hopes are enhanced by today's conjunction between the Sun and Jupiter. The extremely fortunate planetary combination makes this a splendid time for personal enjoyment, happy encounters and pleasure in the company of your good friends. Even strokes of bad luck occurring now will actually turn out for the best… giving a better result than if nothing had happened in the first place. Don't hide your light under a bushel now. The louder you sing your own praises, the more you'll be appreciated.

FRIDAY, 2ND APRIL
Mercury direct

The movement of Mercury into direct motion always brings periods of muddle and hesitation to a welcome end. If you have lost valuable bits of paper or misplaced your house keys, you can expect all these to be returned to you now. If your car has been off the road, it should be back on its wheels again and in fine fettle soon. If you have been vaguely fed up, your usual optimism will return.

CANCER

SATURDAY, 3RD APRIL
Moon conjunct Mars

Your emotions are swinging up and down wildly at the moment and your mood will go from being deliriously happy to becoming quite depressed or even extremely angry. Events will come at you with the speed of arrows and, while some of them will be just what you most want, others will be the last thing you need. Take care if using machinery or anything to do with fire today, because your attention span isn't what it should be and you could hurt yourself.

SUNDAY, 4TH APRIL
Mercury sextile Venus

Your yearning for excitement and adventure is infectious today. A journey in company with one or more of your friends will be a riot. Plenty of laughs are to be had, so don't stick to the tried and true, follow your instincts to the new and different. You'll love it!

MONDAY, 5TH APRIL
Moon sextile Neptune

If you've been prone to any stress-related complaints, you should see an improvement today. Pressure in your life seems to be easing now, and it wouldn't do to take on too much just as things are getting better.

TUESDAY, 6TH APRIL
Saturn square Neptune

The sadness in the life of a friend could get you down today. You may feel sorry for this person while realizing that there is nothing you can actually do to help the situation in a practical manner. You can of course give emotional support, and that may be all that is required.

WEDNESDAY, 7TH APRIL
Sun sextile Uranus

You are keen to get something important off the ground today and to take up a new undertaking. This may require a sort of revolution in your usual thinking, because it looks as though your usual methods won't really apply in this case. You may have to learn something new, a new technique of some kind, or you may have to struggle with a new piece of machinery at your place of work.

THURSDAY, 8TH APRIL
Moon sextile Mars

Close partnerships may have been suffering from inadvertent neglect. Today's aspect between the Moon and Mars gives you a chance to remedy that situation. If you're honest, you'll agree that both of you are in need of some excitement to add a little spice to your relationship.

FRIDAY, 9TH APRIL
Moon sextile Mercury

If you suggest a holiday or an unusual trip to your other half today, you will be delighted by his or her response. Any ideas which you talk over with others now will be well received, even if they are rather new and revolutionary. If you have any kind of legal or official matters on your mind now, this too will begin to work in the way you want. Even outright enemies will lay off for a while.

SATURDAY, 10TH APRIL
Moon square Saturn

You may come up against sticky situations of an official or governmental kind. Something really irritating, such as a parking fine is a distinct possibility! You could be invited to serve on a jury or to arbitrate in some other unpleasant manner in connection with something that has nothing to do with you personally.

SUNDAY, 11TH APRIL
Moon sextile Sun

You may be faced with a bit of a battle today but your confidence is high and you seem to have an inner conviction that you can win. To be honest, we think that you are quite right!

MONDAY, 12TH APRIL
Venus into Gemini

As Venus enters your Solar house of secrets and psychology, it is obvious that the next few weeks will increase the importance of discretion in your romantic life. You'll find that it'll be wise to draw a veil over the more intimate side of your nature, and you'll be less inclined to confide your deepest secrets even to your closest friends. Quiet interludes with the one you love will be far more attractive than painting the town red just now.

TUESDAY, 13TH APRIL
Moon sextile Venus

The call of the new is very evident today since you'd do nearly anything just to have a change. You'd be off around the world like a shot if you could manage it. This scenario is unlikely just at the moment, but you can still inject a little of the exotic into your life even if it's only a Chinese meal!

CANCER

WEDNESDAY, 14TH APRIL
Moon into Aries

The Moon enters your Solar house of ambition encouraging you to think about the direction of your career. For many tomorrow will bring a resolution to get out of your particular part of the rat race and get stuck into something more fulfilling. Those who intend starting up in business will find plenty of encouragement for your ambitious schemes.

THURSDAY, 15TH APRIL
Moon conjunct Jupiter

This should be a very lucky day of the career scene. Your charm will win friends in high places, and past efforts will not go unrewarded as the Moon conjuncts Jupiter now. Of course, it's important not to exaggerate about your abilities, or to deny past errors. If you can avoid these pitfalls, this will be a day of fortunate advancement.

FRIDAY, 16TH APRIL
New Moon

The new Moon today shows the great heights that you could possibly attain. The message is that there's nothing to fear except fear itself. Reach for the stars and you've got it made. Your career should begin to blossom now and over the next month or so you can achieve the kind of respect and status that you are looking for.

SATURDAY, 17TH APRIL
Mercury into Aries

Your job will take precedence today and you must make an effort to get your voice heard. Fortunately, this will not be too difficult because your superiors and your colleagues will be reasonably ready to hear what you have to say. You may have some bright ideas in other areas of life today as well, and you shouldn't hesitate to put these into practice.

SUNDAY, 18TH APRIL
Moon conjunct Venus

You really are a soft touch today, so much so that you must avoid being taken for a ride by others. The people you help may be trying it on, or in some other way trying to shift the responsibility for living their lives or paying their debts onto to you. A friend may whisper secrets into your ear today and you will have to respect their confidence in you by keeping these to yourself from now on.

CANCER

MONDAY, 19TH APRIL
Mars opposite Saturn

One can't expect an easy day when Mars opposes Saturn, and when this unfortunate combination occurs in areas associated with leisure and friendships, one can't really expect these to go smoothly either. Frayed tempers and irritable people will be far too common today.

TUESDAY, 20TH APRIL
Sun into Taurus

As the Sun makes its yearly entrance into your eleventh Solar house, you can be sure that friends and acquaintances are going to have a powerful influence on your prospects. The Sun's harmonious angle to your own sign gives an optimism and vitality to your outgoing nature. Social life will increase in importance over the next month. You'll be a popular and much sought after person. Obstacles that have irritated you will now be swept away.

WEDNESDAY, 21ST APRIL
Venus opposite Pluto

You'll be prone to unfounded fears today since your emotional state is rather insecure. You'll imagine all sorts of disasters, but that doesn't make any of them real! Don't over-react to a minor disappointment in love.

THURSDAY, 22ND APRIL
Mercury sextile Neptune

You will be able to see ways forward both in terms of ambition and in money-making potentials today. The combination of Mercury and Neptune gives you the insight and the ability to make your inspirations work to your maximum benefit.

FRIDAY, 23RD APRIL
Jupiter sextile Uranus

A stunning stroke of luck is forecast by the splendid aspect between Jupiter and Uranus. A professional opportunity may come out of the blue, or equally likely you could receive a cash windfall. All travel arrangements and foreign contacts will benefit you.

SATURDAY, 24TH APRIL
Sun opposite Mars

This is one where the temper is too close to the surface for comfort. The wrong word could get a reaction far out of proportion to the offence. Humour is distinctly thin on the ground now, and woe betide anyone who makes light of a serious issue around you! Lazy people too are likely to irritate you to distraction!

SUNDAY, 25TH APRIL
Moon trine Saturn

People who, through no fault of their own, abandoned education at an early age or did badly at school may wish to put right the gap in their knowledge and qualifications. Though the Lunar aspect to Saturn makes you painfully aware of your deficiencies, you shouldn't feel that you are unintelligent! There's always a change to make good a bad situation. Do something practical about furthering your academic career now.

MONDAY, 26TH APRIL
Mercury trine Pluto

Good news on the job front is set to arrive today. This could alter your perceptions of what is possible and encourage you to aim higher up the career ladder than you had previously thought possible. The sky's the limit!

TUESDAY, 27TH APRIL
Sun conjunct Saturn

This is a strange day in which you may find yourself running into old friends or people you used to work with in the past and this will take you down a path of reminiscence and of happy memories. There could be another equally odd event which propels you into the future in a big way. You could meet new people and make new friends who will have a strong influence on your future ideas and decisions. A day to remember.

WEDNESDAY, 28TH APRIL
Moon opposite Mercury

You may not be able to think straight today and you could get yourself into something of a muddle either at home or at work. The trick to surviving this kind of planetary aspect is to keep to the most mundane and routine of tasks and to take plenty of breaks. Don't bother with anything that requires acuity or clarity of mind until the stars have moved on a bit.

THURSDAY, 29TH APRIL
Mercury sextile Uranus

It's obvious that you are highly thought of in your place of work, but when it becomes obvious exactly how highly you are regarded, it may come as something of a shock. A boost to your income and your self-confidence go hand in hand today.

CANCER

FRIDAY, 30TH APRIL
Full Moon

Your creative soul and romantic yearnings come under the influence of today's Full Moon, so it is time to take stock of those things in your life that no longer give any emotional satisfaction. Children and younger people may need a word or two of advice now and the love lives of all around you will become the centre of interest. You're own romantic prospects may see an upturn too.

May at a Glance

LOVE	❤	❤	❤	❤	❤
WORK	★	★	★		
MONEY	£	£	£	£	
HEALTH	✪	✪	✪	✪	
LUCK	∪	∪	∪		

SATURDAY, 1ST MAY
Mercury conjunct Jupiter

The wheel of fortune turns in your favour today with the conjunction of Mercury and Jupiter. Mists have cleared from your vision and you can again see the enormous potential open to you. For many the planetary link will create professional connections with foreign countries. For others there could be the chance of a new, more fulfilling job or a promotion in the offing. This is an excellent day for attending interviews, writing to potential employers and talking over plans with those who can use their influence to advance your schemes.

SUNDAY, 2ND MAY
Moon sextile Neptune

You will find that you are easily influenced by the views and actions of others today, and will be quite prepared to follow their lead especially in work and monetary dealings.

MONDAY, 3RD MAY
Moon sextile Uranus

You may hit upon an idea for something that makes you look and feel better. You may discover the regenerative powers of evening primrose oil, ginseng or some other miracle cure. You may find something good to eat or some kind of beauty product that clears your complexion or makes you feel better. Even if there is nothing new for you to try, treat yourself to a luxurious soak in your favourite bubble bath and relax.

TUESDAY, 4TH MAY
Moon opposite Venus

If your approach to health care involves lots of tasty treats and a somnolent spell stretched out on the sofa, that's all very well, but you know your body needs a spot more physical exercise and discipline to keep it in tip-top shape. Dietary indulgence is your particular bugbear, and today you need to be more than usually vigilant or you'll find your hand in that biscuit tin before you realize it!

WEDNESDAY, 5TH MAY
Mars into Libra

Your energies will be directed to your home and the area around it. Thus you may spend time working on or in the home or on the land around the place today. If the dishes are piling up in the kitchen, then get down to washing them up and if you haven't a clean shirt or a pair of socks to match, then get around to doing the washing now. Mars in the domestic area of your life over the next few weeks could bring a rash of plumbers, builders and all kinds of other domestic workmen your way.

THURSDAY, 6TH MAY
Moon square Jupiter

Though you may be oozing self-confidence today, it isn't wise to provoke any confrontations unless you are absolutely sure that you are in the right. Examine your own viewpoint or you'll not only regret hasty words but you could be humiliated into the bargain. Don't blithely assume that you'll have back-up, because you'll find that even those you trust will question your motives.

FRIDAY, 7TH MAY
Neptune retrograde

Neptune turns to retrograde motion today and that will bring a few muddles and misunderstandings in connection with money and partnerships. This is a bad time to get involved with other people in any kind of business arrangement and it is a very bad time to lend money to anybody. This is also a bad time to get involved sexually with anybody, especially if you don't know them very well!

CANCER

SATURDAY, 8TH MAY
Mercury into Taurus

The swift-moving planet Mercury enters your eleventh Solar house today and gives a remarkable uplift to your social prospects. During the next few weeks you'll find yourself at the centre point of friendly interactions. People will seek you out for the pleasure of your company. This is also a good time to get in contact with distant friends and those you haven't seen for a while. The only fly in the ointment is that you shouldn't expect a small phone bill.

SUNDAY, 9TH MAY
Mercury sextile Venus

It's rare that Mercury and Venus get far enough apart to make an angle to each other but that's the case today, and this astral event heralds a boost to your social life, your capacity to make new friends and your personal charm. What more do you need?

MONDAY, 10TH MAY
Moon square Pluto

You seem to be fed up with your usual routine and the thing that is getting you down the most at the moment is your job. You may feel the need for a change of job or even a complete change of direction now. Guard against being manipulated by others now and don't allow the machinations of a strong and determined adversary to cost you your job or anything else that is yours.

TUESDAY, 11TH MAY
Mercury square Neptune

You must be careful today because the mixed rays of Mercury and Neptune confuse issues abominably. The unwise words of a friend could be taken as gospel truth which will lead you up the garden path. Anything begun today may be abandoned when common sense returns.

WEDNESDAY, 12TH MAY
Moon trine Pluto

You seem to have made a lot of efforts to get your chores done recently and now you will see the results of all this. Your superiors at work will be happy with your work and, more importantly, you will be happy with your endeavours. There could be a pay rise in the offing or some kind of bonus, either directly as a result of what you have been doing recently or just as a matter of routine. Either way, it will be very welcome.

THURSDAY, 13TH MAY
Mercury conjunct Saturn

Be careful about what you say now because you could find yourself being bound by your own words in a way which becomes inconvenient later on. On the other hand, if you have thought out what you are going to say beforehand and you know that you will be happy with the results, then go ahead and speak your piece. Friends, especially those who are older or who are in positions of responsibility could be very helpful now.

FRIDAY, 14TH MAY
Moon sextile Venus

Something will turn out to be a very pleasant surprise today and it may just be that this is the day that you meet the love of your life. Even if that is not the case, you will be a great success socially and you could even be the hostess with the mostest! You seem set to cause a sensation wherever you go and you will definitely be at the top of everybody's popularity list!

SATURDAY, 15TH MAY
New Moon

There's no doubt that issues surrounding friendship and trust are very important now. The New Moon in your horoscopic area of social activities ensures that encounters with interesting people will yield new and enduring friendships. Though your mood has tended to vary between optimism and despair recently, the New Moon can't fail to increase your confidence and vitality.

SUNDAY, 16TH MAY
Venus sextile Saturn

If you are single and are keen to meet someone to love, then today's events could be extremely interesting and also very important to you in the long run. The reason for this is that a friend could be instrumental in introducing you to someone who will become part of your future. For those of you who are already in committed relationships, you may make a good new friend today.

MONDAY, 17TH MAY
Mercury square Uranus

You could find yourself in a very irritating position today. If there's one thing you hate above all others, it is waiting for someone else to make up their mind. Secretiveness also proves frustrating since you can't get a straight answer to a straight question.

TUESDAY, 18TH MAY
Moon sextile Saturn

You are on the right track, and other people will soon confirm this for you. Older people could be quite helpful to you now, either in connection with some kind of official matter or in respect of something of a social nature.

WEDNESDAY, 19TH MAY
Moon square Jupiter

Be realistic today! That's the astral message now, as a strong influence of Jupiter encourages you to take an overly optimistic view of nearly everything. You could take on far more than you can comfortably handle in a work situation now.

THURSDAY, 20TH MAY
Moon opposite Neptune

This is not a good day to get involved in any kind of money matter. Don't gamble today and don't agree to any kind of joint venture that involves money. Don't lend money to anyone today either. Try not to buy anything important or to sign anything important today either because it will turn out to be an expensive mistake if you did so.

FRIDAY, 21ST MAY
Sun into Gemini

The Sun moves into your house of secrets and psychology today making you very aware of your own inner world of dreams and imagination. For the next month you'll be very aware of the hurdles that face you, and all those things that tend to restrict your freedom; however your imagination and almost psychic insight will provide the necessary clues to overcome these obstacles. Issues of privacy are very important for the next few weeks.

SATURDAY, 22ND MAY
Uranus retrograde

The retrograde course of Uranus may shake the financial markets today. However you shouldn't over-react to an apparent threat to your financial stability. Wait to see what happens before you change any of your cash arrangements.

SUNDAY, 23RD MAY
Mercury into Gemini

You'll find yourself in a more introspective mood for a few weeks because Mercury, planet of the mind, enters the most secret and inward-looking portion of your horoscope from today. This is the start of a period when you'll want to understand the inner being, your own desires and motivations. Too much hectic life will prove a distraction now so go by instinct and seek out solitude when you feel like it.

MONDAY, 24TH MAY
Moon trine Mercury

A talk with a family member will led to a greater understanding of each other's viewpoint. Previous domestic tensions can now by put aside as a harmonious atmosphere prevails. Many of the issues that have divided you will seem trivial beside this heart-to-heart. If differences can't be totally resolved, at least you'll agree to differ now.

TUESDAY, 25TH MAY
Sun trine Neptune

If you are keen to investigate psychic or occult matters, this is a good time to do so. Your intuitive powers are on a high just now and, if you wanted to join a seance or learn to be a medium or a spiritual healer, there could hardly be a better time to do so. You may be drawn towards astrology too, especially the more personal kind of astrology where you learn to make up and to interpret a birthchart.

WEDNESDAY, 26TH MAY
Sun conjunct Mercury

The Sun and Mercury move into close conjunction today which heightens your imagination to the point of pain. It would be too easy to get carried away with an idea now and let baseless fears rule your life. You're quite emotional now, so when the light of reason is overwhelmed by your ego, your anxieties come to the fore. Don't be taken in by flights of fancy.

THURSDAY, 27TH MAY
Moon square Neptune

This isn't the best day to concentrate on anything too important. Your judgement is likely to be rather flawed and it would be too easy to make some serious financial mistakes. The trouble is that your emotions are colouring your judgement and it will be difficult to think logically.

FRIDAY, 28TH MAY
Moon square Uranus

Prepare for the unexpected today for the Moon and Uranus are astrally set to stir up a hornet's nest of complications. This is going to be a confusing day when you won't know where you are in any emotional context. Children especially may be rebellious and troublesome but if you over-react you could make a minor irritation into a full-scale war. Try to keep your cool.

SATURDAY, 29TH MAY
Mars opposite Jupiter

Concentrate on getting your act together at home and at work now because, although things may be a bit quiet today, they will soon take off once again at a rate of knots. Keep your eye firmly on your goals and aspirations because you will rarely get better opportunities for advancement. Romance will come as a result of being in the public eye, so don't sit at home hiding behind closed doors.

SUNDAY, 30TH MAY
Full Moon

Something is coming to a head in relation to your job. This is not a major crisis and there is absolutely no need to flounce out of a perfectly good job, but there is a problem that should be solved before you can continue on in a happy and peaceful frame of mind. You may have to sort out what your role is and which part of the job other people should be doing, because it looks as if you are carrying too much of the load at the moment.

MONDAY, 31ST MAY
Venus square Mars

Keep your mind on what you are doing in and around the home today. Mars is badly aspected and this could bring silly accidents while working around the place. It is a poor day for getting on with home improvements, decorating, dressmaking or fancy cooking. It would be better either to go out and get on with jobs elsewhere or simply to relax and forget the chores for once.

June at a Glance

LOVE	❤	❤	❤		
WORK	★	★	★	★	★
MONEY	£	£	£	£	£
HEALTH	✚	✚	✚	✚	✚
LUCK	♘	♘	♘	♘	

CANCER

TUESDAY, 1ST JUNE
Venus square Jupiter

Though it's important to keep up a healthy ego it's not too wise to rub in your superior knowledge and experience to all those around you. You are well aware of your potential and talents now but you really don't want to upset the applecart by showing off. You could so easily alienate potential allies when it would be so much better to win friends with a display of a little more charm and modesty.

WEDNESDAY, 2ND JUNE
Sun opposite Pluto

It is hard to work out who is in charge of whom today. You may feel that your position is being undermined but you could also be trying to put one over on someone who, theoretically, is in charge of your department. If you don't go out to work, then there could be accusations about who does or doesn't do what in the home.

THURSDAY, 3RD JUNE
Mars direct

You have had to put a good many plans aside lately, especially in connection with your home and family but the planets are suggesting that you get these plans out of storage once again and put them into action. It may be that you have discarded some ideas as being unworkable, but now there will be an opportunity to find others and to put them into operation. Your energy level will be higher from now on too.

FRIDAY, 4TH JUNE
Mercury trine Mars

A secret is likely to be confided to you today. It would be in your best interests to keep this piece of information to yourself since it could involve a skeleton in your family's closet.

SATURDAY, 5TH JUNE
Venus into Leo

Your financial state should experience a welcome boost for a few weeks as Venus, one of the planetary indicators of wealth, moves into your Solar house of possessions and economic security from today. You feel that you deserve a lifestyle full of luxury now and that'll be reflected in the good taste you express when making purchases for your home. Your sense of self-worth is boosted too which might indicate a renewed interest in high fashion.

SUNDAY, 6TH JUNE
Moon square Pluto

You may be off-colour today or you may be overwhelmed with work. Either way, this is not the best of days in which to get anything done and it would be worth knocking off early and spending the evening resting. You may find that others are being manipulative or even completely untruthful to you today, so don't take too much notice of them. Have an early night tonight.

MONDAY, 7TH JUNE
Mercury into Cancer

The movement of Mercury into your own sign signals the start of a period of much clearer thinking for you. You will know where you want to go and what you want to do from now on. It will be quite easy for you to influence others with the brilliance of your ideas and you will also be able to project just the right image. Guard against trying to crowd too much into one day today.

TUESDAY, 8TH JUNE
Sun trine Uranus

A period of solitude and deep thought would do you no harm at all, and would clarify some of the unexplained events that you've experienced recently. Take it easy today and give yourself time to adjust to new circumstances.

WEDNESDAY, 9TH JUNE
Moon sextile Uranus

There may be some unexpected help on its way to you, especially in connection with your career or your aims and aspirations. If you have been struggling with a tricky problem for a while, a friend may be able to help you solve it in a trice.

THURSDAY, 10TH JUNE
Venus opposite Neptune

Guard against unnecessary spending today because anything that you buy now is unlikely to turn out to be much of a bargain. Women friends will lead you in the wrong direction today so try to rely upon your own judgement rather than that of your female friends. Women colleagues may be vague and peculiar in some way today.

FRIDAY, 11TH JUNE
Moon square Uranus

It would be a very bad idea to get involved in any kind of get-rich-quick scheme with friends or acquaintances at the moment. It may be worth taking what others tell you with a rather large pinch of salt today. You may be torn between the needs of your family and the demands of your pals today and it may be impossible to please both sets of people at once.

SATURDAY, 12TH JUNE
Moon trine Neptune

Unseen forces seem to be working in your favour now and you could find yourself getting on much better in life than you have been able to do for some time past. You may have friends in high places who are beavering away on your behalf now. You could just as easily attract the attention of a new and exciting lover now, simply by being in the right place at the right time. The message here is that you don't have to work hard at anything to make it work today.

SUNDAY, 13TH JUNE
New Moon

The world of romance is especially attractive on a day when your dreams and fantasies take over your life. The New Moon points the way to new emotional experiences in the future, but you mustn't cling to the past because of misplaced loyalty or guilt. Some people are leaving your life, but if you were honest you'd admit that they're no real loss. Follow your instincts now and your dreams may well come true.

MONDAY, 14TH JUNE
Venus trine Pluto

Money is coming your way! Of course, some effort has got to go into it, but once you see the potentials of a new scheme you'll be straining at the bit to get started. A highly profitable period is forecast by today's aspect between Venus and Pluto.

TUESDAY, 15TH JUNE
Mercury sextile Saturn

There's a calm, controlled atmosphere today as you talk over your plans with a close friend. A more mature point of view will go a long way to clarifying certain personal issues now. If you ask for advice, listen to what you receive. It may not be what you want to hear, but you can be sure it's for the best.

WEDNESDAY, 16TH JUNE
Sun trine Mars

Some big plans may have to be put on hold for a while simply because you haven't got the cash resources to back them up. Though that's the sensible solution I doubt that you'll be too keen for any delay to creep into your well thought-out schemes. Therefore you're likely to be very active today looking for alternative sources of finance. Self-employed people will have considerable ingenuity in dealings with accountants and banks.

THURSDAY, 17TH JUNE
Moon opposite Uranus

However much you try to save money, it seems to be drifting out of your grasp today. However sensible you try to be, the fates just won't let you hang on to what you have got. So, you are likely to be tempted by a new suit of clothes, a set of sports gear or an item for the home this week. Electrical goods may catch your eye and tug at your credit card, musical CDs will call you and, by the end of the day, you will even have arranged for the decorators to come in.

FRIDAY, 18TH JUNE
Moon trine Jupiter

Your highly developed intuition is detecting a financial problem in your life at the moment and that requires some serious thought. You've got a chance to sort out what you should do in both your job and in money matters now. Keep following the hunches and you'll be led to a remarkable opportunity.

SATURDAY, 19TH JUNE
Venus square Saturn

You may feel that you don't fit into a group situation now and that you will have to leave and go it alone for a while. The reason may be that your values and priorities are not the same as those of the rest of the group. Your hopes and dreams will have to take a back seat for the time being because this just doesn't seem to be the best time to push forward with them. You may be a bit short of money today too.

SUNDAY, 20TH JUNE
Sun sextile Jupiter

The intuition hits an almost psychic level now as the Sun powerfully influences Jupiter. Career worries and financial complications may prove an obstacle course but you can chart your way with ease if you allow your deepest feelings to guide you. Keep following your hunches today and you won't go wrong.

MONDAY, 21ST JUNE
Sun into Cancer

The Sun moves into your own sign today bringing with it a lifting of your spirits and a gaining of confidence all round. Your birthday will soon be here and we hope that it will be a good one for you. You may see more of your family than is usual now and there should be some socializing and partying to look forward to. Music belongs to the realm of the Sun, so treat yourself to a musical treat soon.

T U E S D A Y , 2 2 N D J U N E
Venus opposite Uranus

Don't rely on luck today. Your financial fortunes will be due for a dip if you give in to temptation and gamble on anything! The same goes for investments. If you must go in for HP or other long-term money deals read the small print very carefully indeed. Better still, leave such things for another day!

W E D N E S D A Y , 2 3 R D J U N E
Mercury square Mars

There seems to be a certain amount of pressure being placed upon you from the domestic area. This may manifest itself in the form of a practical problem in the home or to do with your home. If you have a small business, there could be something wrong there. Feelings may be running high all around you, and your own nerves seem to be rather stretched by all these problems.

T H U R S D A Y , 2 4 T H J U N E
Moon opposite Saturn

You may find yourself out of sympathy with other members of the family who belong to different generations. It may be your parents or your in-laws who get you down today or it may be the children who are being impossible. There is very little opportunity for escape and freedom seems as far away as it does for a 'lifer' sitting in his lonely cell. You are short of time for yourself and that is the problem, really.

F R I D A Y , 2 5 T H J U N E
Mercury square Jupiter

Being folk who are constantly urging positive thinking, it is hard for us to say that optimism is a very good thing as long as it isn't taken too far. Today's stressful aspect between Mercury and Jupiter is a case in point. Though your view of the career picture is extremely promising, aren't you relying a just a little too much on luck? Has your balanced perspective been replaced by wishful thinking? Try to keep your feet on the ground today.

S A T U R D A Y , 2 6 T H J U N E
Mercury into Leo

All the planets seem to be restless just now since Mercury changes sign today. At least you can get your mind into gear concerning the state of your finances now. Tasks you've been putting off like cancelling useless standing orders, or ensuring you receive the most advantageous interest from your savings will be tackled with ease now.

SUNDAY, 27TH JUNE
Moon trine Venus

If you get stuck into the chores today, you will get them done in no time at all. So, if you have been putting off some boring job of work either at home or at your place of work, get it out of the way for good and all today. You may push yourself a bit too hard today, but we all do this from time to time and today is your day for being the world's greatest workaholic.

MONDAY, 28TH JUNE
Jupiter into Taurus

The trials and tribulations of the past few months are fading away rapidly now and you can begin to enjoy the lighter side of life once again. Your sense of humour will come bubbling back up the surface again and there will soon be plenty for you to laugh and joke about. Your best bet is to keep yourself in the swim by joining clubs, societies or groups of people who share your interests.

TUESDAY, 29TH JUNE
Moon trine Saturn

A suggestion made by your spouse or indeed a close friend should be heeded today. This comment will have a wealth of common sense in it, and is not one that you can afford to ignore.

WEDNESDAY, 30TH JUNE
Mercury opposite Neptune

Lock away your cheque book, hide your credit cards and keep away from the shops. Money is likely to slip through your fingers like water today if you aren't careful. This wouldn't be so bad if you had something to show for it; unfortunately you're unlikely to get anything of real value for your cash.

July at a Glance

LOVE	♥	♥	♥	♥	
WORK	★	★	★	★	
MONEY	£	£	£		
HEALTH	✪	✪			
LUCK	♘	♘	♘	♘	♘

THURSDAY, 1ST JULY
Moon sextile Pluto

Anything that you do with a partner should turn out to be very successful today. The possibilities are many and varied because they may run from tackling some kind of major do-it-yourself task with your partner to setting up a business deal with a real wheeler-dealer. Finances that are connected to business matters will also go well today.

FRIDAY, 2ND JULY
Moon opposite Venus

Don't be taken in by attractive offers or apparent bargains today, because you'll find that for every cent saved you'll pay a dollar in repair bills. Shoddy goods and glib promises are the main dangers so don't allow yourself to be gullible or to fall for attractive packaging. Equally, a desire to spend beyond your means should be curbed immediately.

SATURDAY, 3RD JULY
Moon trine Mars

With your sensitivity a little more under control, you're back to being an exciting soul today. It wouldn't take much for you to take off in search of some adventure. So much the better if you can find an amusing companion to share in the experience. This could turn out to be an extremely romantic interlude.

SUNDAY, 4TH JULY
Mars opposite Jupiter

The world is your oyster today – at least, that's how it seems. Though you are pretty exuberant, you mustn't fool yourself into believing that wishful thinking is fact! In affairs of the heart especially, your expectations should not ignore common sense. Try to keep your feet on the ground.

MONDAY, 5TH JULY
Mars into Scorpio

Your desires suddenly become very strong indeed as Mars changes sign, and temptations will tend to sweep you up without a single thought about the consequences. If the path of true love doesn't run smoothly, it's not for want of passionate intensity on your part. The one thing to watch for is that you'll tend to move so swiftly that you're prone to minor cuts and bruises. Take it easy.

TUESDAY, 6TH JULY
Moon square Sun

There could be some kind of power struggle going on today. In practical terms, this could bring you up against an authority figure or someone who has a rather high degree of self-regard. This could also make things difficult for any business dealings that you have on the go at the moment. However, on a less practical note, you may doubt your own judgement for a while.

WEDNESDAY, 7TH JULY
Moon trine Venus

Attend to practical matters today and deal with anything to do with money now. If you talk to your bank manager about finances for a business idea, you will get some really useful advice and, most probably, all the help you require to go along with this. If you need to save up for some kind of future event or a future project, then set this in motion soon.

THURSDAY, 8TH JULY
Mercury trine Pluto

A work colleague will make a financial suggestion that you'd be wise to follow. It may not be anything startling in itself, just another way at looking at an old problem that enables you to turn it to your advantage. A long-term debt may be resolved at this time.

FRIDAY, 9TH JULY
Moon square Venus

A friend could let you down today and the chances are that the friend in question is a female one. Those of you who are dating a potential lover could find that your arrangements to meet one another go wrong today or, worse still, that you get off on the wrong foot with each other in some way. An awkward day.

CANCER

SATURDAY, 10TH JULY
Moon sextile Mercury

Keep a few matters to yourself today. Even if a friend or a neighbour tries to worm things out of you, try to keep your mouth firmly shut. Your financial position is improving rapidly now but it would be a good idea to keep this information to yourself just at the moment because there are plenty of people around you who would be only too happy to relieve you of any extra pennies that you may have put by.

SUNDAY, 11TH JULY
Mars square Neptune

You are prone to strong and somewhat irrational desires today, but do try to be sensible all the same! Temptation may be ever-present but you'd be a fool to spend your hard-earned cash in indulging your whims. If you do fall prey to these impulses, then regrets will surely follow!

MONDAY, 12TH JULY
Mercury retrograde

It's typical, just as Mercury was getting to grips with your financial state, the wayward planet backtracks sending all cash affairs into chaos once more. At least this is a temporary problem. However, you'll have to take extra trouble to be completely clear in financial matters. Check all facts and figure thoroughly just to be on the safe side.

TUESDAY, 13TH JULY
New Moon

There's a New Moon in your own sign. This is a powerfully positive influence that encourages you to make a new start and personal opportunities are about to change your life. You must now be prepared to leave the past behind to embark on a brand new course. Decide what you want, because you'll be your own best guide now.

WEDNESDAY, 14TH JULY
Moon conjunct Mercury

Get your bank statements and cheque books out and work out what you have or have not got in hand for your current expenses. You seem to be in the mood to deal with all those boring financial details and perhaps this is no bad thing. After all this bookkeeping and secretarial work, why not pour yourself an expensive drink and celebrate being in the black or commiserate with yourself for being in the red once again!

CANCER

THURSDAY, 15TH JULY
Venus trine Jupiter

Invite all your fine friends to a party today or, if this is too complicated to arrange at short notice, then get together with them in the nearest pub or restaurant and enjoy a gossipy get-together. Convivial conversation surrounds you and the connections you make while socializing could turn out to be useful to you in other ways later on.

FRIDAY, 16TH JULY
Mercury trine Pluto

A word to the wise is said to be sufficient – especially when cash is concerned! So when Pluto and Mercury combine forces subtle hints are coming your way that you'd do well to note. Keep these to yourself though or others will jump on the profitable bandwagon too!

SATURDAY, 17TH JULY
Void Moon

The Moon is 'void of course' today, so don't bother with anything important and don't start anything new now. Stick to your usual routines and don't change your lifestyle in any way.

SUNDAY, 18TH JULY
Saturn square Uranus

You will feel constrained by other people's expectations of you at the moment and will long to break free of a boring set of circumstances. This may not yet be possible; however any thought of delay will cause you to seethe inwardly.

MONDAY, 19TH JULY
Moon trine Uranus

This is likely to be a very active day. You are mentally on top form so problems and worries can be easily sorted out now. There is also an indication of openness between yourself and a partner so any big decisions should be talked over now while there is still time. You'll find that someone close has some good workable ideas that can be put in practice for the benefit of all. Don't keep things to yourself today.

TUESDAY, 20TH JULY
Moon square Sun

It's a difficult day emotionally simply because you feel a sense of unease that's hard to pin down. The outlook isn't improved by the harsh Lunar aspect to the Sun, which sets your nerves on edge and gives a restlessness that's hard for you or indeed anyone else to live with. Your own four walls are pressing in on you now. You need some space so get out and about. Relatives, especially older females will tend to irritate by not giving you any credit fort intelligence.

WEDNESDAY, 21ST JULY
Jupiter square Neptune

Apparent strokes of luck will be anything but today! Jupiter and Neptune combine forces to blinker your perceptions and lead you up the garden path. Be sceptical when a friend makes outrageous promises.

THURSDAY, 22ND JULY
Mercury square Mars

There could be considerable tension between you and the younger members of the family now. They may be going that bit too far and taking your good nature for granted or being thoughtless or careless in some way. Ask yourself if what you want of them is reasonable and, if the answer is yes, then insist on it. You may find that your lover doesn't share your priorities today and this could also cause a bit of tension.

FRIDAY, 23RD JULY
Sun into Leo

Your financial prospects take an upturn from today as the Sun enters your house of money and possessions. The next month should see an improvement in your economic security. It may be that you need to lay plans to ensure maximum profit now. Don't expect any swift returns for investments but lay down a pattern for future growth. Sensible monetary decisions made now will pay off in a big way.

SATURDAY, 24TH JULY
Moon sextile Uranus

A sudden and unexpected event will help you to make a success of something that you are doing at work. If you don't go out to work, then you could acquire some kind of machinery that helps you to get through the chores at home. A friend will come up with some good ideas and he or she will be a source of help and support both at home and at work.

SUNDAY, 25TH JULY
Mercury square Jupiter

Your intentions may be good but you must also have your head screwed on the right way round. Therefore, if you intend to get involved with any kind of business venture or money matter with friends, then make sure that this is on a totally professional footing right from the start. Working partnerships should also be kept on a strictly business footing for the time being.

MONDAY, 26TH JULY
Sun opposite Neptune

This is likely to be a rather grim day on the financial scene. The Sun is opposed to Neptune which is not a good situation for your cash flow. Overspending is likely or the consequences of past indulgence. Be careful that you don't make plans without having the ability to pay for them.

TUESDAY, 27TH JULY
Sun square Jupiter

Don't allow your idealism to get out of control. It is all very well wanting to help every lame duck or to heal the world but your purse strings will only stretch so far. You're so full of optimism that you will be tempted to take on tasks that are beyond your capacity to cope with physically or financially. Be realistic about what you can and cannot do for yourself and others.

WEDNESDAY, 28TH JULY
Full Moon eclipse

There is an eclipse of the Moon today which will affect two areas of your life in a rather profound way. Firstly, it may be that your job is going through a patch of turbulence now and this may even bring you close to making a change of some kind. It may be worth waiting until the dust has settled a bit before making any sweeping changes. Your health may let you down now too and, if so, don't leave things to chance.

THURSDAY, 29TH JULY
Moon square Saturn

You seem afflicted by an aura of gloom today. It is all the fault of the Lunar aspect to Saturn which puts a damper on anything that would usually please you. Money could be the area that you blame most for this grim mood. Brighten up! It can't possibly be as bad as you think!

FRIDAY, 30TH JULY
Sun trine Pluto

Your organizational abilities will be awe-inspiring today. A work project that has suffered from a weak-willed approach will benefit from your shrewd restructuring. Your grasp of finances will also come in very handy.

SATURDAY, 31ST JULY
Mercury into Cancer retrograde

Whenever Mercury is in retrograde motion life becomes muddled and at the moment, this is exactly what is happening to you. You may find it hard to get your head round all the decisions that you have to take and, when you ask others for advice, they either won't want to be bothered with you or they won't have anything useful to say to you.

August at a Glance

LOVE	❤	❤			
WORK	★	★			
MONEY	£	£	£	£	
HEALTH	✚	✚	✚	✚	✚
LUCK	♘	♘	♘		

SUNDAY, 1ST AUGUST
Moon trine Mercury

You should hear from people who are at a distance from you now and there could be an invitation on the way for you to visit far-flung family members or friends who have retired to sunnier or more restful spots. You may be asked in a roundabout way if you would like to work abroad. Another possibility is that someone could make you a job offer based on the way you think or on some specific area of your knowledge.

MONDAY, 2ND AUGUST
Moon trine Sun

It is rare that you're in such an efficient and practical frame of mind, but today you could take on the professional world and win through. In financial and career matters the positive aspect between the Moon and Sun promises a highly successful time. Your more unusual insecurity is nowhere to be seen as you display an organizational talent that might even be a surprise to you!

TUESDAY, 3RD AUGUST
Venus trine Jupiter

A good day for romantic journeys – because any journey can be romantic when you are in the company of the one you love. It's a time of jollity, self-indulgence and fun.

WEDNESDAY, 4TH AUGUST
Moon trine Venus

A chat with a woman friend may be just the thing to help you get things into perspective today. You seem to need some kind of practical advice in order to prevent you from taking a rather foolish course of action. A pal may suggest an unexpected and rather unusual outing later in the day and you would be missing a lot of fun if you turned this down.

THURSDAY, 5TH AUGUST
Moon conjunct Saturn

Though you usually have no patience with petty rules and mind-numbing red tape, you can today handle the most complex document with ease. Half the battle is won when you know your rights, so don't be put off by irritating officials, or long-winded forms because they'll be no match for your ingenuity and persistence. Legal affairs can be safely dealt with now because you have a superb eye for detail, not to mention a homing instinct for a loophole!

FRIDAY, 6TH AUGUST
Mercury direct

At last, Mercury turns tail and starts to move forward, bringing to an end a period of confusion or mental frustration that has had you in its grip for the last two or three weeks. You can embark on serious negotiations with others now if needs be and you can move ahead with all kinds of business matters. Any trips which have been delayed can now be taken and muddles and mishaps will soon be cleared up.

SATURDAY, 7TH AUGUST
Sun square Mars

Keep that fiery temper under control today. The Sun's harsh aspect to Mars makes it too easy to blow minor financial concerns out of all proportion. You may even think that you're being reasonable; unfortunately those around you will know that's not the case. Try to address worries sensibly rather than taking out your frustrations on those who would support you given half the chance.

CANCER

SUNDAY, 8TH AUGUST
Sun opposite Uranus

Watch your spending today. There may be something that catches you out and causes you unexpected expense of some kind. If you decide to buy something on impulse today, it is likely to work out badly. A bargain won't be a bargain today, that's for sure. Avoid making complicated plans that involve the co-operation of friends today because that won't work either.

MONDAY, 9TH AUGUST
Moon sextile Saturn

A serious discussion with a friend will show that you aren't the flippant person that you often pretend to be. You will understand your friend's circumstances simply because you've been in the same position previously.

TUESDAY, 10TH AUGUST
Sun square Saturn

You are definitely up against it at the moment and the issue seems to be one of respect and authority. Thus, you may find yourself being badly treated by someone in authority or by someone who is unwilling to show you a reasonable amount of respect for what you do. You yourself may be demanding more than others are willing to do, and you will have to ask yourself whether you are being reasonable or not.

WEDNESDAY, 11TH AUGUST
New Moon eclipse

If Nostradamus is right, there won't be many people left to read the rest of this book after today! However, we're more optimistic even though there is a new Moon eclipse in your Solar house of personal finances and personal possessions. This will bring a problem to a head in connection with money, land, property or goods that belong to you. There are many ways that this could affect you but one possibility is that you have some kind of dispute over who owns what.

THURSDAY, 12TH AUGUST
Mercury into Leo

Mercury's timely entry into your financial sector should be a great help to your situation. Your mind will now be clear and you can see all issues from a logical standpoint. Now you'll be able to budget sensibly, pay off outstanding debts and generally make sense of your cash flow. The shrewdness that Mercury brings to bear on your economic life will enable you to control income and expenditure.

CANCER

FRIDAY, 13TH AUGUST
Mercury opposite Neptune

This is not a day when you should sign on the dotted line for anything! Avoid hire-purchase agreements, leave insurance policies well alone and don't be taken in by smooth-talking salesmen! For some reason you are blind to financial pitfalls just now so play safe!

SATURDAY, 14TH AUGUST
Mars opposite Saturn

Though you fancy having some fun, many of your friends are too caught up in their own worries to be good companions. This could be a rather frustrating day since no one else seems willing to join you in a frivolous mood.

SUNDAY, 15TH AUGUST
Venus into Leo retrograde

The return of Venus to your area of money and possessions gives you another chance to look at the financial realities and sort them out. If you aren't careful now you could get yourself into debt or otherwise tie up your resources for no good purpose.

MONDAY, 16TH AUGUST
Moon sextile Sun

Home life and comfort move to centre stage today as the Moon makes a positive aspect to the Sun. All those luxuries that you crave may come a step nearer today, as you realize that you can afford to treat yourself. Perhaps some new furniture is in the offing.

TUESDAY, 17TH AUGUST
Mercury square Jupiter

It would be too easy for you to be talked into parting with your cash for the benefit of someone else today. It is certainly not a time to be taken in by sob stories or to lend any money to a so-called friend.

WEDNESDAY, 18TH AUGUST
Moon opposite Saturn

You could be bored and irritable today and longing for something interesting to happen. Your usual sources of amusement don't seem to interest you now and your friends and family are either uncooperative or busy with their own interests just now. Someone may annoy you by interfering with your usual routine or trying to 'supervise' your life or your work in some way.

CANCER

THURSDAY, 19TH AUGUST
Pluto direct

After a longish period of travelling retrograde, Pluto now moves to direct motion and this will help you to make sense of a number of things that have been bothering you recently and then to put these right. You may, for example, have been fighting against a confusing and worrying situation in your place of work recently. Another possibility is that your health has not been all that great lately. Either way, improvements are coming now.

FRIDAY, 20TH AUGUST
Sun conjunct Venus

The light at the end of the financial tunnel is promised by today's stars. You're in the right mental state to make some sensible decisions concerning the monetary realities. A plan to increase your profitability should be embraced today because the combined influences of the Sun and Venus promise considerable economic gain. Don't let this positive influence go to your head though, because you'll still tend to overspend.

SATURDAY, 21ST AUGUST
Moon trine Venus

There's nothing quite like it when you feel that you're back in efficient control. The arena for this sense of mastery is the bank balance. You'll be busy with a calculator working out the minutiae of your financial position. There's plenty of satisfaction is this, though to others the obsessive accounting may seem a boring activity. You could find that your economic fortunes are better than you expected.

SUNDAY, 22ND AUGUST
Moon trine Jupiter

If you and your lover get together with friends, you will find that a chat will do much to cheer you both up and also to clear your minds about one or two points. A visit to your local hostelry might be just the place for this. There should be good news about money matters coming your way today and the results of this will be shared between you and your lover.

MONDAY, 23RD AUGUST
Sun into Virgo

Your curiosity will be massively stimulated from today as the Sun enters the area of learning and communication. Other people's business suddenly becomes your own now. That's not to say that you turn into a busybody overnight, it's just that many will turn to you for some guidance. Affairs in the lives of your brothers, sisters and neighbours have extra importance now. Short journeys too are well starred for one month.

TUESDAY, 24TH AUGUST
Venus square Mars

They say that a woman's place is in the wrong! Well, today your place is in the wrong, whatever your gender. You won't be able to please anybody, so try pleasing yourself; at least this way somebody will be satisfied! You may find that other people cost you money or that they take up your time on wild-goose chases or in some other way waste your resources. Younger members of the family will be in a touchy mood too.

WEDNESDAY, 25TH AUGUST
Jupiter retrograde

Just when everything seems to be going along nicely and all that you want is just within your grasp, Jupiter is throwing a spanner in the works. Don't give up, just sit back for a while and wait for better times to come along. This is not a good time to go into a new venture, especially where money is concerned and if you can avoid making any complicated journeys over the next few weeks, it might be just as well because delays are pretty certain.

THURSDAY, 26TH AUGUST
Full Moon

You may have to face the fact that you cannot slope off to distant and romantic shores just now. This doesn't mean that you are forever confined to your home, just that you cannot get away right now. Your mood is not only escapist but also rebellious today! You won't want to have anything to do with people who restrict you or who remind you of your chores and duties but you simply won't be able to escape them.

FRIDAY, 27TH AUGUST
Mercury conjunct Venus

There's nothing that could please you more than a stimulating conversation with people you feel in tune with, in luxurious surroundings. And, if you've got any sense of purpose, that's exactly what you'll arrange for today. You could pick up some financial tips as well.

SATURDAY, 28TH AUGUST
Sun trine Jupiter

You feel the need to talk things over with someone who can take an objective view of you and your life today and, fortunately, just the right person will come along. Such a chat will give you an opportunity to sort out your beliefs and to begin to form a new and more rational philosophy of life. The stars are happy to give the green light to your most idealistic schemes and they will add zest and zeal to most of your ideas.

SUNDAY, 29TH AUGUST
Moon trine Pluto

Today could bring the breakthrough you have been waiting for. There is strong evidence that you are about to reach some kind of objective or to achieve something that you have been striving for. This may be the end of a creative endeavour, the passing of a test of some kind or a promotion at your place of work. Whatever you do or don't do, there is a sense of achievement today and a turning-point feeling to it all.

MONDAY, 30TH AUGUST
Saturn retrograde

A number of areas of your life will tend to slow down for a while now and, in addition to this, you will find yourself having to take on more responsibility. You may find yourself in charge of some kind of group and this may be in connection with work or some part of your social life. If you have to guide and influence others now, you may have to do so the hard way, by putting your foot down.

TUESDAY, 31ST AUGUST
Mercury into Virgo

Your mind will be going at full speed ahead over the next few weeks and you are bound to come up with some really great new ideas. You will be very busy with the phone ringing off its hook and letters falling into your letter box by the ton. You will find yourself acting as a temporary secretary for a while, even if the only person who makes use of your services is yourself.

September at a Glance

LOVE	♥	♥	♥		
WORK	★	★	★	★	★
MONEY	£	£	£	£	£
HEALTH	✚	✚			
LUCK	∪	∪	∪		

WEDNESDAY, 1ST SEPTEMBER
Moon square Venus

A friend may bring you a sob story about needing money or needing to borrow something that you own. If you have any doubts about the truth of this tale, then protect yourself and your goods at the risk of losing this rather dubious friendship. You may join in with some kind of group activity now and this could cost you money or it could clash with other priorities and other calls upon your time.

THURSDAY, 2ND SEPTEMBER
Mars into Sagittarius

The transit of Mars into your area of health and work shows that you must show that you have initiative and drive to make the most out of your prospects now. The energies of the fiery planet won't allow you to sink anonymously into a crowd. You'll be forced to stand out and make your mark on the professional world. In health affairs, the vitality of the planet must be good news. Rarely have you felt so alive and effective. You may find that some colleagues are distressed at this assertion of your personality and aims; unfortunately for them, they'll just have to put up with it!

FRIDAY, 3RD SEPTEMBER
Mercury trine Jupiter

It's time to get together with others and organize a meeting of like-minded people for a particular purpose. Discussions will have a positive outcome and a group would have more real power than any one of its individuals. Signing up for some kind of group activity would be a good idea now and you might consider joining an evening class where you will meet others who share your interests. Something sporty or outdoorsy may appeal to you now.

CANCER

SATURDAY, 4TH SEPTEMBER
Mercury square Pluto

If you don't have to travel today, then thank your lucky stars. If you do, then be prepared for delays, confusions and problems all round. Work may turn out to be something of a problem too today and if you have to travel in connection with your work, then you really ought to consider 'throwing a sicky' today. In other words, tell the boss you aren't well!

SUNDAY, 5TH SEPTEMBER
Moon sextile Saturn

It will be easy to get others to co-operate with you on a creative project today. Your partner will be quite happy to help you out with any personal venture and, if you need any more assistance, try asking parental figures today.

MONDAY, 6TH SEPTEMBER
Mars sextile Neptune

Tasks that you would usually shy away from, become easy today. The energy of Mars will help you to get the most difficult or boring jobs out of the way quickly. You could be surrounded by workmen at some time during the day.

TUESDAY, 7TH SEPTEMBER
Moon opposite Uranus

Avoid getting involved in any kind of strange or unusual financial arrangements today, and you should also avoid lending money to friends or acquaintances. Help a pal out with a few dollars or pounds by all means, because the chances are that the loan will come back to you in some other way but avoid anything that requires large sums of money or large and expensive goods.

WEDNESDAY, 8TH SEPTEMBER
Sun conjunct Mercury

There's no doubt that your mental powers are on top form today. The conjunction of the Sun and Mercury lets your intelligence shine. You are particularly persuasive now too, so it shouldn't be difficult to win even the most stubborn and entrenched person over to your cause.

THURSDAY, 9TH SEPTEMBER
New Moon

The New Moon shows a change in your way of thinking. In many ways you'll know that it's time to move on. Perhaps you'll find yourself in a new company, a new home or among a new circle of friends in the near future. Opinions are set to change as you are influenced by more stimulating people. Perhaps you'll consider taking up an educational course of some kind.

FRIDAY, 10TH SEPTEMBER
Sun trine Saturn

You will be able to get your point of view across today in no uncertain terms. You may be involved with powerful and important people but you will not be nervous in their presence. You know that you are in possession of all the relevant facts and that they will trust and believe you. You may be dealing with personal matters but it is equally possible that you will do all this on behalf of a group.

SATURDAY, 11TH SEPTEMBER
Venus direct

Money should flow into your hands more easily from now on. Venus returns to direct motion and that cannot fail to increase the amount of cash at your disposal. A tasteful but not too expensive purchase will cheer you up at this time.

SUNDAY, 12TH SEPTEMBER
Moon sextile Venus

There are good vibes surrounding your home, family and personal security today. The Moon is in good aspect to Venus showing good fortune is showered on you and yours. Female relatives can expect excellent news.

MONDAY, 13TH SEPTEMBER
Moon square Neptune

Common sense has flown today since your heart definitely rules your head. if you've got the urge to express your love by means of an extravagant gesture, please make sure that it's not going to cripple your bank balance.

TUESDAY, 14TH SEPTEMBER
Moon opposite Saturn

Relationships are the problem area today. Things don't seem to be going too well simply because you may want to spend more time with a friend than you do with your lover. The generation gap may also be a troublesome issue at this time.

WEDNESDAY, 15TH SEPTEMBER
Mars conjunct Pluto

The planets are filling you with energy today and any recent health problems should disappear fast from now on. Changes are coming thick and fast in connection with your work now, and you can expect to be considering a change of career soon. If you don't work at all, you may now consider getting a job and if you are nearing retirement age, you could now consider doing something completely different.

THURSDAY, 16TH SEPTEMBER
Mercury into Libra

The past exerts a powerful influence as Mercury enters the house of heritage. You'll find that things long forgotten will somehow re-enter your life over the next couple of weeks. An interest in your family heritage may develop, or possibly a new-found passion for antiques. Some good, meaningful conversations in the family will prove enlightening.

FRIDAY, 17TH SEPTEMBER
Mercury trine Neptune

This will be quite an easy day and there may be strange and subtle reasons for this. On the face of things, there may be no difference between today and many other days, but you seem to be learning the art of centring yourself and of developing a kind of inner strength that helps you get through things more easily.

SATURDAY, 18TH SEPTEMBER
Moon square Mercury

You may have to put up with some flak from your family or your partner today. There may be muddles and misunderstandings all around you, or they may simply be in a tense and tetchy frame of mind. You may have difficulty in operating machinery of some kind and there will definitely be gremlins in your computer or word processor. This may sound crazy, but if the weather is 'heavy' or there is a chance of lightning, then don't use machinery at all (especially computers) if you can avoid it.

SUNDAY, 19TH SEPTEMBER
Moon trine Saturn

A very practical plan will be presented by your partner or close friend. There may be a lot of work involved, yet this idea is splendid and deserves some serious attention.

MONDAY, 20TH SEPTEMBER
Moon trine Sun

This is a day to be sociable and outgoing. An invitation received now should be accepted at once, no matter what reservations or prior arrangements you have. A meeting with friends and neighbours could lead to a possible romance. If you're already hitched, take your other half on a magical tour of the social scene. Fun and laughs all round.

TUESDAY, 21ST SEPTEMBER
Mercury sextile Pluto

Good news on the job front will boost your self-confidence and rub off on your home life. You'll be eager to tell your nearest and dearest all about the exciting new developments. Family members too will have good news to share.

WEDNESDAY, 22ND SEPTEMBER
Moon opposite Venus

When you make up your mind to buy a gift, there's no point in telling you to skimp on the expense. Shoddy goods just aren't good enough for someone special in your life. The trouble is, will the bank balance actually cope with it? Think twice before you make a grand gesture because you'll find that a simple smile or a kiss would do just as well as the most costly gem… probably better!

THURSDAY, 23RD SEPTEMBER
Sun into Libra

The home and family become your main interest over the next four weeks as the Sun moves into the most domestic area of your chart from today. Family feuds will now be resolved, and you'll find an increasing contentment in your own surroundings. A haven of peace will be restored in your home. This should also be a period of nostalgia when happy memories come flooding back.

FRIDAY, 24TH SEPTEMBER
Mars sextile Uranus

Sudden shocks and surprises are set to shake your workplace today. Mars and Uranus team up to put a rocket under outmoded practices and time-honoured habits! However, form your point of view this is a good thing opening up scope for a greater expression of your talents.

SATURDAY, 25TH SEPTEMBER
Full Moon

Today's Full Moon shows that important decisions have to be made at a time of rapidly changing circumstances. News that arrives today could well be disturbing yet will prove to be a blessing in disguise in the long run. You may be considering a move of home, possibly to a distant location. Or even throwing in your present career to take up an educational course of some kind. People you meet while travelling will have important words to say.

CANCER

SUNDAY, 26TH SEPTEMBER
Moon opposite Mercury

You may have to rush round to see one or other of your parents today. Alternatively, another older member of your circle could need your assistance now. The problem is that the messages that you are being given are a bit muddled and, when you actually look into the reality of the situation, it may be much better (or worse) than you first realized.

MONDAY, 27TH SEPTEMBER
Moon square Neptune

Gullibility is the problem today. The Lunar aspect to Neptune makes you rather susceptible to sob stories, glib liars and con merchants. Take care when even friends spin you a tale. It wouldn't be wise to part with any cash at all right now.

TUESDAY, 28TH SEPTEMBER
Moon conjunct Saturn

Now you will really find out who your friends are because you will have the strength to confront anyone whom you suspect has been less than a good friend to you, in order to sort out what is going on. There may be some really good news in connection with older members of the family or about people who are in positions of responsibility over you. You could also have a good day in some kind of group activity.

WEDNESDAY, 29TH SEPTEMBER
Moon trine Neptune

It's a day for some peace and quiet as far as you're concerned. You can't cope with constant interruptions or demanding people. Lock yourself away, take the phone off the hook and get on with your own business in solitude.

THURSDAY, 30TH SEPTEMBER
Moon trine Uranus

A friend could point you in the direction of a bargain today. He or she could help you in other ways too. For instance, if you need to hire the services of someone to do a particular job for you, either at work or around the home, you friend could know just the right person to help you out.

October at a Glance

LOVE	❤				
WORK	★	★	★	★	
MONEY	£	£	£	£	
HEALTH	✪	✪	✪	✪	✪
LUCK	∪	∪			

FRIDAY, 1ST OCTOBER

Sun sextile Pluto

You could decide to break the habits of a lifetime today, and you'll find that there'll be no better time to do so! Many will consider giving up smoking, taking up a more healthy diet and generally looking after yourself more… and there's nothing wrong with any of that!

SATURDAY, 2ND OCTOBER

Mercury sextile Venus

Your phone will be ringing off its hook and your letter box will be full of news today and, the chances are that all the news is good. There will be invitations to family celebrations and it is possible that there will also be good news about a property matter. If you have been waiting to hear about a potential move of house or any other arrangement concerning money and property, this should be moving in your direction very soon now.

SUNDAY, 3RD OCTOBER

Moon square Mercury

There will be a number of ups and downs today which will have your emotions swinging from one extreme to another. Someone may say something that really upsets you and worse still, makes you doubt yourself. If you talk this over with a friend or a relative, you will find that they are just as outraged as you are at the unpleasant way you have been treated. It's nice to find out who your friends are.

MONDAY, 4TH OCTOBER

Moon sextile Sun

This is an excellent day in which to buy goodies for the home. So, if your curtains need replacing or if the dog has chewed the cushion covers just one time too many, take yourself out to the shops and see what you can do about it.

TUESDAY, 5TH OCTOBER
Mercury into Scorpio

Mercury moves into a part of your horoscope that is concerned with creativity. Mercury rules such things as thinking, learning and communications, but it can also be associated with skills and craftwork of various kinds. The combination of creativity and craftwork suggests that the next few weeks would be a good time to work on hobbies such as dressmaking, carpentry and so on.

WEDNESDAY, 6TH OCTOBER
Sun trine Uranus

This could be your lucky day! Whatever happens, you are in for a few pleasant surprises. You may be asked to make a start on a new and exciting project and this may involve you in a lucrative or a pleasantly enjoyable joint venture of some kind. You may discover that a long-lost uncle has left you a fortune or you may be blessed with a wonderfully useful idea. A day to remember.

THURSDAY, 7TH OCTOBER
Venus into Virgo

If you've got any favours to ask, the passage of Venus into your Solar house of persuasion shows that you can use considerable charm and eloquence to win others over to your point of view with little trouble at all. A little flirtation combined with a winning way ensures that you achieve your desires. Your creative talents are boosted too, so perhaps you should consider writing down your inspirations now.

FRIDAY, 8TH OCTOBER
Moon trine Neptune

There's a touch of deception around at the moment, and you can't blame anyone but yourself. Gossip is rife and the rumours all add up to a totally wrong conclusion. In other words, two and two don't make five! If you're concerned about your security and the future solvency of a firm don't fly into a panic just yet. Have confidence. Your fears are likely to be unfounded.

SATURDAY, 9TH OCTOBER
New Moon

The New Moon falls in the sphere of home and family today indicating a need for a change. For some reason you've been dissatisfied with your domestic set-up so you may consider looking at house prices in your own or indeed another area. You probably feel that you need more space and light in your life than your present home is providing. A family member may be considering setting up home and deserves all the encouragement you can give.

SUNDAY, 10TH OCTOBER
Venus trine Jupiter

Forget your worldly cares and get out and about in the company of friends today. Even a simple shopping trip could turn into an adventure packed with laughs and a chance to pick up a few bargains as well. The strong influence of Venus may hint of romance in the offing too!

MONDAY, 11TH OCTOBER
Jupiter square Neptune

If you encounter a gift-horse today, then open its mouth and have a good look because very little will be as it seems, and strokes of luck will turn out to be anything but in the long run. In other words, be very cautious!

TUESDAY, 12TH OCTOBER
Void Moon

This is not a great day in which to decide anything or to start anything new. A void Moon suggests that there are no major planetary aspects being made, either between planets or involving the Sun or the Moon. This is a fairly unusual situation but it does happen from time to time and the only way to deal with it is to stick to your usual routines and do nothing special for a while.

WEDNESDAY, 13TH OCTOBER
Mercury square Uranus

Don't be alarmed by anything you hear today! Gossip is likely to be inaccurate or a down-right lie! There could be a hidden motive behind this attempt to give you the jitters. Think carefully before you react in any way.

THURSDAY, 14TH OCTOBER
Neptune direct

Neptune turns to direct motion today, and this will make it easier to cope with relationships. You may have been so blinded by love that you haven't seen things clearly, and you may have credited your lover with characteristics that he or she doesn't have. Moreover, you may have been laying all the faults of the world on someone else's shoulders. Neptune's direct motion from now on may help you to understand the truth of the matter a bit more clearly.

CANCER

FRIDAY, 15TH OCTOBER
Moon conjunct Mars

This is a highly energetic and vital day as the Moon conjuncts Mars. It's fast and furious action all the way but at least you've got the physical strength and tenacity to cope with the pressure. In work, if you can keep your head while all around you are losing theirs, you won't be doing too badly at all.

SATURDAY, 16TH OCTOBER
Mercury opposite Saturn

If you thought you could please yourself and indulge your own interests today, the demands of those you know will get in the way of your desires. Duty to others could be a burden now, and won't give you any peace to pursue your own pleasures. The generation gap will seem to be growing wider by the minute as oldsters and children will be particularly irksome.

SUNDAY, 17TH OCTOBER
Mars into Capricorn

Today, Mars moves into the area of your chart that is devoted to relationships. This planetary situation is like a double-edged sword because, on the one hand, it could bring you closer to your partner or loved one while, on the other hand, it can cause you to become extremely angry at the behaviour of others.

MONDAY, 18TH OCTOBER
Venus square Pluto

We wouldn't be surprised if you have a twinge of backache today. Either that or there's an emotional problem that's taking your mind off your work. In both cases the remedy is to take things as easy as possible until the situation rectifies itself.

TUESDAY, 19TH OCTOBER
Moon square Saturn

An old friend may leave your life soon but this parting need not be permanent even though you will feel a keen sense of loss. Remember that nature abhors a vacuum and someone will come along to brighten your mood and fill the gap.

WEDNESDAY, 20TH OCTOBER
Moon sextile Jupiter

If a friend suggests a short holiday, weekend break or just a jaunt to your local shopping centre you should immediately accept. This is your chance to have a lot of fun and encounter some new faces. The more intellectually inclined will benefit too since your interest is bound to be stimulated in social settings.

CANCER

THURSDAY, 21ST OCTOBER
Moon opposite Venus

You aren't on top form emotionally today. In fact, your vulnerability is such that you couldn't put up any resistance to pressure or emotional blackmail now. You'd far rather follow the crowd than stand out in any way. You're very anxious to please, but this is a trait that shouldn't be taken too far. Serious decisions about the state of your relationship will have to be put off until you are feeling stronger.

FRIDAY, 22ND OCTOBER
Sun square Neptune

This is a bad time to make decisions about relationships. Therefore, if you seem to have met the man or woman of your dreams, take some time out before making any promises, because you might be blinded by a rose-tinted infatuation just now. Much the same goes for money-making schemes or creative ideas. Just take everything a step at a time and it will be all right.

SATURDAY, 23RD OCTOBER
Sun into Scorpio

You are going to be in a slightly frivolous frame of mind over the next few weeks and you shouldn't punish yourself for this. Pay attention to a creative interest or a demanding hobby now or get involved in something creative on behalf of others. A couple of typical examples would be to be the production of a school play or making preparations for a flower and vegetable show.

SUNDAY, 24TH OCTOBER
Full Moon

Today's Full Moon could make you feel a bit tetchy and tense and it could also bring you some sort of unexpected expense. The best thing to do today is to stick to your usual routine and not start anything new or important. Jog along as usual and try not to become caught up in anybody else's bad mood now.

MONDAY, 25TH OCTOBER
Venus trine Saturn

A much needed chat with an older friend will clarify your emotional state today. If you've been torn between duty and pleasure you'll find that there is time for both now. A sense of commitment is evident in all your relationships whether they be platonic or romantic in nature.

TUESDAY, 26TH OCTOBER
Moon opposite Mercury

You may hear some disappointing news today, possibly in connection with a friend or with children and youngsters. You may have to cancel plans connected to these people, either because they can't join you today or because you are too busy elsewhere to be bothered with them.

WEDNESDAY, 27TH OCTOBER
Moon opposite Pluto

The aspects today are much the same as for the first day of the month, therefore take a rest from the chores if you can. Work will prove to be difficult to get through and it would be better to leave large or awkward tasks for a day or two at least. You may find women particularly irritating today and you may even feel a bit under the weather now. Rest and relax as much as you can.

THURSDAY, 28TH OCTOBER
Mercury sextile Neptune

Words of love are music to your ears today. You are deeply sentimental and rather soft now, so the one thing you want is for someone close to tell you how much you mean to them. Creatively too, you are on top form. All artistic endeavours, especially the written word, will be successful.

FRIDAY, 29TH OCTOBER
Moon opposite Mars

This is a tense and touchy day and you won't improve matters by acting like a bull in a china shop. If you start throwing your weight around and handing out orders to your nearest and dearest, you are likely to provoke an unpleasant response. It is true that you want to improve your marital and business partnerships now but you need to bear in mind that these are subtle and sensitive relationships.

SATURDAY, 30TH OCTOBER
Mercury into Sagittarius

The movement of Mercury into your Solar sixth house of work, duties and health suggest that a slightly more serious phase is on the way. Over the next three weeks or so you will have to concentrate on what needs to be done rather than on having a good time. You may have a fair bit to do with neighbours, colleagues and relatives of around your own age group soon and you will have to spend a fair bit of time on the phone to them.

SUNDAY, 31ST OCTOBER
Moon square Sun

Go easy on your expenditure today. Avoid the shops, don't go looking for bargains and don't let anybody else talk you into buying anything either. Older relatives may be a bit irritating today, possibly because they need you to do something for them which eats into your spare time. It would be better to spend today attending to your duties rather than to seek out amusements.

November at a Glance

LOVE	❤	❤	❤	❤	
WORK	★	★	★	★	
MONEY	£				
HEALTH	✛	✛	✛	✛	✛
LUCK	⋃	⋃	⋃	⋃	⋃

MONDAY, 1ST NOVEMBER
Void Moon

Today is one of those odd days when there are no important planetary aspects being made, not even to the Moon. The best way to tackle these kinds of days is to stick to your usual routine and to avoid starting anything new or tackling anything of major importance. If you do decide to do something large today, then it will take longer and be harder to cope with than it would normally.

TUESDAY, 2ND NOVEMBER
Moon square Mercury

It's a very tense outlook today for the Moon and Mercury put your nerves on edge. Of course, your own anxieties will prove to be far more exhausting than any outside influence in your life just now. If you're wise you'll avoid challenges today and indulge in some relaxation. If you do insist on facing up to every little thing that the world throws at you, you'll end up depleted and glum.

WEDNESDAY, 3RD NOVEMBER
Moon trine Saturn

This is an excellent time to embark on something unusual or off-beat. It is also a good time to start on something which is, in any sense of the word, educational, with long-term projects being better starred than short-term ones. If you are in contact with parents or parental-figures, then it would be a good idea to give them a ring today because you should hear something from them or about them that pleases you greatly.

THURSDAY, 4TH NOVEMBER
Moon sextile Mercury

Good news! If you are waiting for something to be fixed at home or at work, it will be. Frustrations will melt away as friends, neighbours and relatives rush round to help out with all those minor chores and problems that are plaguing you. A neighbourhood event may provide some unexpected amusement and pals who pop in may provide some more.

FRIDAY, 5TH NOVEMBER
Moon trine Uranus

You and your partner could decide to spend some money on domestic refurbishment now. If you are involved in a small business, especially any kind of shop, this will go well now. Selling things for charity will also succeed today, as will dealing with the public for any purpose. Even if you customers are difficult, you will sail through the lot with no problem at all.

SATURDAY, 6TH NOVEMBER
Sun opposite Saturn

A socially awkward situation could get you and a loved one at loggerheads today. The main cause of this is pure embarrassment, either on your part or your lover's. Either way, it won't solve anything to make a scene.

SUNDAY, 7TH NOVEMBER
Sun sextile Mars

This is a good day for pleasure and romance. The playful atmosphere of the last few days continues as the Sun aspects your ruler Mars. Now, though you have innate vitality and enthusiasm for life. You may feel you want to make a casual emotional link into something more permanent. You could sweep a lover off his or her feet.

MONDAY, 8TH NOVEMBER
New Moon

There's a New Moon today casting a glow over your artistic potential. Your talents should shine now so have some belief in yourself and in what you can offer to the world at large. Of course if art and literature leave you cold, you may be more inclined to an amorous path. Conventional values are not for you now since you're determined to be yourself and to chart your own course. Make time to have fun, you deserve it.

TUESDAY, 9TH NOVEMBER
Mercury into Scorpio

Serious concerns should be the last thing on your mind as Mercury enters your Solar house of fun and leisure from today. Jokes, witty quips and a display of eloquence will make you one of the most popular people around. Creatively speaking, Mercury also enhances more general powers of communication so you should consider setting down your thoughts in a lasting form. Creative writing whether prose or poetry would fulfil an instinct to express your talents.

WEDNESDAY, 10TH NOVEMBER
Moon sextile Uranus

If you've been feeling under the weather, the energizing influence of Uranus should soon improve that situation. The same goes for any problems at work as a new set of circumstances sweeps away old irritations.

THURSDAY, 11TH NOVEMBER
Moon trine Jupiter

You may lack self-belief but those around certainly don't. In fact, they think that you could do far better for yourself and ascend heights undreamed of. Try to match their belief in you with a little more confidence in your own abilities. Dealings with people in a position of authority will go well, better in fact than you expect.

FRIDAY, 12TH NOVEMBER
Moon square Venus

This could be a stressful day if you don't give yourself enough space for a breather. The Moon's harsh aspect to Venus points out that there are a thousand and one things to do around the home, but if you're wise you'll put a few of the more difficult ones off till another day. The same goes if you are being nagged. Try to explain patiently that everything will be done – just give it time.

SATURDAY, 13TH NOVEMBER
Moon conjunct Mars

Something important concerning relationships must be tackled over the next few weeks and you and your lover will be putting extra energy into your relationship.

This may be in the form of taking up a sporting hobby or some other kind of shared interest now or you may simply decide to see a bit more of each other. Business or working partnerships will benefit from this planetary movement too.

SUNDAY, 14TH NOVEMBER
Saturn square Uranus

Financial problems and friends who seem to think you are made of money are your main problems today. You will feel the urge to break out of a rut but seem unable to do so at the moment. To put it bluntly – your patience will be at a very low ebb!

MONDAY, 15TH NOVEMBER
Moon square Saturn

It would be easy to plunge into a pit of gloom today since you'll assume that a friend has rejected you. Of course this isn't true, it's just that your pal has got a life too, and personal matters must take priority at the moment.

TUESDAY, 16TH NOVEMBER
Mercury sextile Mars

You'll be a silver-tongued charmer today, with enough sex appeal to drive anyone wild with desire. You can use your seductive wiles to good advantage because no one could possibly resist you.

WEDNESDAY, 17TH NOVEMBER
Venus sextile Pluto

Deep feelings are aroused today as a situation arises within your family that is reminiscent of one that occurred a long time ago. This is not such a bad thing, since you have now learned how to deal with this simply by referring to past experience. Apart from that, the aspect of Venus to Pluto should be good news for your love life.

THURSDAY, 18TH NOVEMBER
Moon trine Mercury

There is a youthful atmosphere around you today, and this means that you could spend the day with younger members of your family or that you could help out at a school event of some kind. You will be amazed at the depth and openness of youngsters' minds and you could be quite inspired by their ideas. You may try your hand a new sport or game now.

CANCER

FRIDAY, 19TH NOVEMBER
Moon sextile Neptune

Your sensitive handling of a delicate situation will find favour with bosses and other authority figures today. This could be an opportunity for career advancement or a raise of some kind.

SATURDAY, 20TH NOVEMBER
Venus trine Uranus

If you have recently been through a rather trying time when everything and everyone seemed to be against you, today will bring a nice change of atmosphere. Friends will drop by and they will be happy to give a hand in sorting out any minor domestic crisis that comes your way today. Your partner may have happy news to impart, and everybody else who is around you seems to be in a good mood today.

SUNDAY, 21ST NOVEMBER
Mars square Jupiter

The encouraging career picture could tempt you into a display of arrogance and conceit that will leave your partner in life feeling like a totally useless accessory. Mars' harsh aspect to Jupiter causes you to overstate your case and possibly make outrageous claims about your achievements. If this is intended to make someone else feel small, then you should be ashamed of yourself. Ask yourself where would you be without someone to lean on?

MONDAY, 22ND NOVEMBER
Sun into Sagittarius

The Sun moves into your Solar sixth house of work and duty for the next month. This Solar movement will also encourage you to concentrate on your health and well-being and also that of your family. If you are off-colour, the Sun will help you to get back to full health once again. If you have jobs that need to be done, the next month or so will be a good time to get them done.

TUESDAY, 23RD NOVEMBER
Full Moon

Apart from a slightly frustrating Full Moon situation today, there is not much going on in the planetary firmament. The best thing to do is to stick to your usual way of doing things and to avoid starting anything new or important. If you feel off-colour or out of sorts, then take whatever medicines you need and try not to work too hard.

CANCER

WEDNESDAY, 24TH NOVEMBER
Moon trine Venus

The finer things of life have a delightful appeal today. You're in a cultured frame of mind susceptible to refined music and fine art. There's also a romantic side to this Venusian influence, so this is a time to indulge yourself in pleasure.

THURSDAY, 25TH NOVEMBER
Sun sextile Neptune

Things are changing, especially at work and in business relationships. Problems that seemed to be totally intractable are now beginning to melt away, and better times will surely come along soon. However, there is one little problem that you must be aware of and that is your occasional habit of seeing things as you want them to be rather than as they are. So keep your eyes open.

FRIDAY, 26TH NOVEMBER
Mars into Aquarius

Mars moves into your Solar eighth house today, raising the level of your feelings to some kind of fever pitch. Your passions will be aroused in some important way and you could find yourself behaving in an unusual manner due to the depth of your emotions. Make sure that you are not simply reacting out of anger or out of some kind of feverish response to anything today.

SATURDAY, 27TH NOVEMBER
Moon opposite Neptune

It's not a good time to sign up to anything too complicated or legal. Hire-purchase agreements and loan arrangements should be left to another day. If you must sign on the dotted line today, then read all small print very carefully indeed.

SUNDAY, 28TH NOVEMBER
Moon square Mercury

You may not feel much like it but today, you need to look into your financial situation and work out a sensible budget for the future. So get out those bank statements and look at your credit card statements and be honest with yourself before you find yourself right off the financial rails. You may feel like going out and enjoying yourself today but duty calls and, therefore, it doesn't look as if you achieve this.

MONDAY, 29TH NOVEMBER
Mars conjunct Neptune

If you follow your intuition today, you won't go far wrong! Two areas are particularly sensitive now. In financial affairs you can pick up on subtle undercurrents and act on the information immediately to your eventual profit. In more personal affairs, intimate secrets and hidden passions will come to light.

TUESDAY, 30TH NOVEMBER
Moon trine Saturn

Talking to an older friend will help you to get many of your ideas into perspective today. An unbiased view from a person of experience will help to sort out many of your problems.

December at a Glance

LOVE	❤	❤	❤	❤	❤
WORK	★				
MONEY	£	£	£	£	£
HEALTH	✚	✚			
LUCK	U	U	U		

WEDNESDAY, 1ST DECEMBER
Venus opposite Jupiter

Ambition hits new heights today as your mind is filled with dreams of incredible worldly success and domestic bliss. That though is the trouble since some of your dreams are so far-fetched that they have no realistic chance of fulfilment. Members of your family do have their feet on the ground yet can't bring themselves to point out the flaws in your plans.

THURSDAY, 2ND DECEMBER
Moon sextile Sun

If you need to get through some chores in and around your home, this is a good day to do so. Do-it-yourself jobs, tidying up, cooking, cleaning and gardening will all go well and make you feel that you have had a really useful day.

FRIDAY, 3RD DECEMBER
Moon opposite Jupiter

It's too easy to get carried away with your own enthusiasm today. Your family too is full of big ideas which you should be trying to temper; unfortunately you are in too much of a state of high excitement to be realistic. With everyone egging the others on it's hard to get a grip on reality today. Don't underestimate the hard work needed to ground your dreams in reality.

SATURDAY, 4TH DECEMBER
Moon square Neptune

It's not a day to gamble, to take a chance or to reveal secrets! The Lunar aspect to Neptune shows that anything covert or even slightly criminal is to be avoided.

SUNDAY, 5TH DECEMBER
Venus into Scorpio

This is a good day to begin new projects and to get great ideas off the ground. Venus is now moving into the area of your chart that is concerned with creativity, so over the next few weeks you can take advantage of this and get involved with some kind of creative process. Venus is concerned with the production of beauty, so utilize this planetary energy to enhance any of your creations now.

MONDAY, 6TH DECEMBER
Sun sextile Uranus

Surprises abound at home and at work. Your lover could have some wonderful news for you today while your employer or employees could surprise you by showing a touching faith in your abilities. You could have a good deal of fun with friends now, especially if you get involved in some kind of charitable or fund-raising venture.

TUESDAY, 7TH DECEMBER
New Moon

Today's New Moon gives you the stamina to shrug off any minor ailments that have been troubling you. Occurring, as it does, in your Solar house of health and work, it's obvious that you need to get yourself into shape to face the challenges that await you. A few early nights, a better diet and a readiness to give up bad habits such as smoking, will work wonders.

WEDNESDAY, 8TH DECEMBER
Venus square Neptune

The heart definitely rules the head today. In fact, it could be said that common sense has flown! You are likely to be swept away by the most unlikely passions and unrealistic dreams. When it comes to love or money, it wouldn't be wise to commit yourself to anything today.

CANCER

THURSDAY, 9TH DECEMBER
Moon sextile Venus

A sparkling aspect between the Moon and Venus will make this a most romantic day. If you have been looking for someone to love, you could find the right candidate today. So, whatever your circumstances, try to make this the most pleasant and affectionate of days for you and your loved ones.

FRIDAY, 10TH DECEMBER
Mars square Saturn

Don't get involved in other people's disputes today. You may think that you are helping out, but you'll only end up getting the blame from both sides for sticking your nose in. Do yourself a favour and leave them to it!

SATURDAY, 11TH DECEMBER
Mercury into Sagittarius

Some monetary worries should be alleviated by Mercury's change of sign today. Of course, this does not come without effort and you may find that you have to take on a part-time job in the short term to get the books to balance. More generally, improvements in the job stakes are now possible, but you'll have to be keenly aware of the possible competition and prepared to act instantly to get the employment you want.

SUNDAY, 12TH DECEMBER
Mercury sextile Neptune

Follow a money hunch today and you are likely to be a winner. The combination of Mercury and Neptune makes you a very perceptive individual, well placed to make your mark on the world. If you have to sell yourself or a money-making idea, your eloquence and obvious belief in your project will earn success.

MONDAY, 13TH DECEMBER
Moon sextile Sun

You are in tune with your innermost self today. Whether you are involved in your daily round of duties or involved with the most complicated forms and financial arrangements you are clear-sighted and totally capable. Even with the most intimate matters, your tact, diplomacy and sense of inner truth will untangle the most complex knot.

TUESDAY, 14TH DECEMBER
Mars conjunct Uranus

You won't be in the mood to put up with any nonsense or arbitrary orders today!

Mars and Uranus urge you to break free of all restrictions and to follow your own instincts. Petty dictators wont know what they're letting themselves in for if they face up to you!

WEDNESDAY, 15TH DECEMBER
Venus opposite Saturn

You may feel like being carried away on a fluffy white cloud of romance but harsh reality is likely to intrude. Reality may come in the form of some straight talking from a friend or two and, while you may not want to hear what they are telling you, in your heart of hearts you will have to admit that they are probably right. Children may turn out to be an obstacle to your dreams in some way.

THURSDAY, 16TH DECEMBER
Moon sextile Neptune

The professional world is looking more promising especially if you can put some of your stunning insights before people in authority. Your ideas will be accepted and you will receive the rewards that you deserve.

FRIDAY, 17TH DECEMBER
Sun trine Jupiter

This should be a glorious day because the Solar aspect to Jupiter ensures good fortune and worldly progress. This also pretty good for physical health. Any ailments that you have suffered from should now improve.

SATURDAY, 18TH DECEMBER
Mercury conjunct Pluto

Subtle persuasion is your forte today. You could convince bosses and work colleagues that black was white, if you were so inclined. Behind this silver-tongued charm there is a stark purpose. You'll be determined to get your own way, and since direct methods aren't likely to work, some soft soap and manipulation should do the job.

SUNDAY, 19TH DECEMBER
Moon conjunct Saturn

This is a good day for dealing with official or governmental people of any kind. You may have to phone your local tax office or your local council and it is possible that you may be asked to help in some kind of governmental or committee matter now. Older people will be particularly kind and helpful and, if you have older relatives to deal with, they will be in a pretty good mood too.

CANCER

MONDAY, 20TH DECEMBER
Jupiter into Aries

The opportunities for career advancement are pretty good for the next year or so. Jupiter moves into the sector of your horoscope that governs status, prestige and business success now, bringing all the optimism and exuberance of the planet to bear on your worldly fortunes now.

TUESDAY, 21ST DECEMBER
Moon opposite Pluto

What you want and what you have to do are two very different things. You feel a deep and abiding need to escape from the world and all its problems but providence and circumstances are preventing you from doing so. You must concentrate on what you are doing and where you are going at work. Even if you don't work, matters regarding duties and obligations must be faced and dealt with now.

WEDNESDAY, 22ND DECEMBER
Sun into Capricorn

The Sun moves into the area of your chart devoted to relationships from today. If things have been difficult in a partnership, either personal or in business, then this is your chance to put everything back into its proper place. It's obvious that the significant other in your life deserves respect and affection and that's just what you're now prepared to give. Teamwork is the key to success over the next month.

THURSDAY, 23RD DECEMBER
Full Moon

Today's Full Moon urges you to let go of the past in some way. You may feel that a total revamp of your image is called for especially if you've got a new love in your life. Old-fashioned attitudes should go the same way as an outmoded outfit. You could also take this opportunity to re-examine some traditional points of view that no longer fit current circumstances. This could herald the birth of a whole new you.

FRIDAY, 24TH DECEMBER
Venus square Mars

There seems to be some kind of hitch in your love life at the moment and it is hard for you to get the kind of togetherness with your lover that you want. Some of you may decide now that your current partnership is no longer viable and thus start to make plans for a solo existence in the future. If there is an unwanted suitor hanging around you now, you will finally find a way to tell him or her that you don't want them near you any more. Not the best Christmas Eve on record!

SATURDAY, 25TH DECEMBER
Moon trine Pluto

Even though it's Christmas Day your mind will range across far-reaching money-making schemes. This renewed positivity could have something to do with an improvement in health which helps you see the long-term picture and be more optimistic.

SUNDAY, 26TH DECEMBER
Mercury sextile Mars

You're a shrewd operator today. Complex financial affairs can't get the better of you and neither can officialdom or red tape. You've got the measure of all opposition and have the brain and the brawn to deal with all of it!

MONDAY, 27TH DECEMBER
Mercury trine Jupiter

You're luck is in today as Mercury and Jupiter open doorways of opportunity. If you bring your powers of persuasion to bear on those who matter, it will soon become obvious to them that you are a person of vision and experience.

TUESDAY, 28TH DECEMBER
Moon square Mercury

You'll find yourself in a daydream for much of the day. If escaping from a boring routine isn't possible, you'll find some release in fantasy. Having said that, it isn't true that fantastic thoughts are a waste of time. You may find that your creativity is stirred by this and will want you to set some of your ideas down. Who knows, this could be the start of a best-selling novel or film script. Don't deny yourself the pleasure of dreams today.

WEDNESDAY, 29TH DECEMBER
Moon square Sun

Sometimes it's the best course to put your own concerns on the back burner and give all your attention to the feelings of a partner or family member. Be generous with your time today and you'll soothe away fears and dreads that your loved one has been harbouring. Be prepared to listen and console. You'll be amply repaid in a renewal of affection.

CANCER

THURSDAY, 30TH DECEMBER
Mars sextile Jupiter

Don't be taken in by appearances. That's the message when Mars and Jupiter point the way to professional and financial success. The obvious trappings of wealth won't appeal at the moment, and those who put a lot of store by them aren't people who will be of any help now. If you use your instincts, you'll find that you have more earning potential than any of the show-offs you once envied.

FRIDAY, 31ST DECEMBER
Venus into Sagittarius

Venus moves out of the fun, sun and pleasure area of your chart into the work, duty and health area on the last day of 1999. This suggests that any problems related to work and duty will become easier to handle in 2000 and also that you could start to see some kind of practical outcome from all that you have been doing lately. Happy New Century!